vegetarian times

FAST AND EASY

Great Foods You Can Make in Minutes

The Editors of *Vegetarian Times*

WILEY

Wiley Publishing, Inc.

Published by Wiley Publishing Inc., Hoboken, NJ

Library of Congress Cataloging-in-Publication Data:
Vegetarian times : fast and easy / the editors of Vegetarian times.
    p. cm.
  Includes index.
  ISBN 978-0-470-08552-3 (pbk.)
  1. Vegetarian cookery. 2. Quick and easy cookery. I. Vegetarian times.
  TX837.V4272 2008
  641.5'636—dc22
                     2007011317

Photographs: Renée Comet and Jacqueline Hopkins
Interior text design: Holly Wittenberg
Cover design: Suzanne Sunwoo

Manufactured in the United States of America

10 9 8 7 6 5 4 3 2 1

table of contents

acknowledgments

The editors of *Vegetarian Times* are indebted to the following people for making this book possible: photographers Renée Comet and Jacqueline Hopkins; recipe developer Fiona Kennedy; nutrition consultant Antonina Smith; and copy editor Robin Cheslock.

We are also grateful for the continued support of literary agent Mary Ann Naples and editor Anne Ficklen, who know that putting together a cookbook is neither fast nor easy, but the delicious result is worth the wait.

Carla Davis
Project Manager

introduction

Quick, delicious and healthful recipes—your busy life demands them. Now you can have the best at your fingertips with *Vegetarian Times: Fast & Easy*, the latest cookbook from *Vegetarian Times*, the leading authority on the vegetarian lifestyle. In these pages you'll find 200 mouth-watering meatless dishes to make again and again: Thai Rice Pancakes, Grilled Sweet Potato Salad, Smoked Tofu Farfalle Casserole and Carrot-Raisin Waffles, to name a few. All are packed with fresh, seasonal ingredients and lots of vegetarian staples such as grains, legumes and tofu. And all can be made in less than 45 minutes. Really!

You'll love not only the familiar favorites but also the recipes you never thought you'd see in a "quick" vegetarian cookbook.

How to use this book

We've made it super-straightforward to plan how long you'll need to be in the kitchen, whether you're hosting a dinner party, packing your kids' lunch boxes or whipping up dessert for a potluck. All of our recipes are clearly marked with icons denoting how long the recipes take to make—with no hidden prep, cooking or cooling times:

15 minutes or fewer

30 minutes or fewer

45 minutes or fewer

You'll find 15-, 30- and 45-minute recipes in each chapter. There's no more guesswork!

About our recipes

After each recipe, we provide nutritional information, including calories, protein, fats, carbs, cholesterol, sodium, fiber and sugars. When a choice of ingredients is given (as in "skim milk or soymilk"), the analysis reflects the first ingredient listed (skim milk). When there's a range of servings (as in "1 to 2 tablespoons olive oil"), the analysis reflects the first number listed (1 tablespoon). When an ingredient is listed as optional, it's not included in the nutritional analysis.

Many of our recipes are vegan, denoted with the VEGAN icon. Vegan means they don't include any animal products, such as eggs, cheese, milk, butter or honey. Most non-vegan recipes can be adapted with your favorite substitutes.

We've also included color photographs of 16 recipes to use as guides. As always, we encourage you to experiment.

The quick cook's pantry

Quick cooking is a snap when you have all the ingredients on hand. Here's what to keep in your pantry:

- Whole-grain breads, such as sandwich and artisan breads, English muffins and tortillas
- Rice, including conventional or quick-cooking brown rice and white rice, such as basmati or jasmine rice
- Whole grains, such as barley, bulgur, cornmeal, rolled oats, millet, quinoa and kasha
- Pasta, preferably whole grain
- Whole-grain cold cereals
- Whole-grain flours, including whole wheat flour, whole wheat pastry flour and other favorites
- Unbleached all-purpose flour
- Legumes (dried or canned), including kidney beans, black beans, navy beans, cannellini beans, chickpeas, lentils and other favorites
- Condiments, such as soy sauce, vegetarian Worcestershire sauce, mustard (Dijon and American), dark sesame oil, pickles, jellies and other favorites
- Sweeteners, such as honey, brown rice syrup, granulated sugar cane juice, molasses, confectioners' sugar, brown sugar and granulated sugar
- Vanilla, almond and lemon extracts
- Baking powder
- Baking soda
- Arrowroot, cornstarch or other thickener
- Vinegars, such as balsamic, red wine and rice
- Vegetable oils, including olive and canola oils
- Salt, including kosher salt, sea salt and seasoning salts
- Peppercorns, whole, for freshly ground black pepper
- Herbs and spices
- Beverages, including fruit and vegetable juices

Basic kitchen equipment

Investing in the best you can afford pays off with each use. Keep these kitchen standards close at hand:

- Pots and pans with lids
- Large skillet, preferably nonstick
- Steamer basket
- Griddle
- Baking dishes and baking sheets
- Wooden cooking spoons and other utensils
- Box grater
- Measuring cups and spoons
- Vegetable peeler
- Large colander
- Small and medium-sized strainers and sieves
- Kitchen scissors
- Blender
- Food processor
- Immersion blender

Tips for quick cooking

Here's how to beat the clock, time after time:

- Set out all ingredients and utensils you'll need before you begin cooking, and mentally walk through your recipe so you can complete tasks simultaneously. For example, while the pasta is cooking, you can mince the garlic for the sauce.

- Keep your kitchen organized. Stash frequently used utensils next to the stove, and store pots and pans within easy reach (a hanging pot rack is great for this). Return everything to the same place when you're done.

- Use prepared and prepackaged foods. Stock your fridge and pantry with frozen and canned vegetables, canned beans, bagged and cut-up produce and canned low-sodium vegetable broths.

- Embrace shortcuts. Quick-cooking and microwaveable grains allow you to skip time-consuming steaming and soaking. Look for rice, barley, bulgur, quinoa and couscous.

- Cut vegetables into small, thin pieces; they'll cook faster than thick ones.

- Make twice as much food as you need, and freeze and refrigerate the leftovers to eat later in the week. There's nothing faster than not having to cook! Simply reheat and serve.

- Take advantage of time-saving gadgets and small appliances, such as food processors, tabletop grills, and microwave ovens.

Why go meatless?

Vegetarian meals are delicious *and* good for you. Four of the top seven causes of death—heart disease, cancer, stroke and diabetes—are related to the typical American diet. Are you concerned about cholesterol? Soy foods and meat substitutes, which are staples in vegetarian cooking, won't stress your cardiovascular system. And people with food allergies and lactose intolerance will love how they feel after filling up on healthful whole grains, vegetables, fruits and legumes.

Keeping your weight down, living longer, building strong bones and reducing the risk of food-borne illnesses are just a few of the other benefits of the vegetarian diet. Because natural and organic foods have gone mainstream, it's easier than ever to find what you need to make meatless meals your whole family will love—and you'll love to make.

So what are you waiting for? Get cooking!

1

Breakfast and Brunch

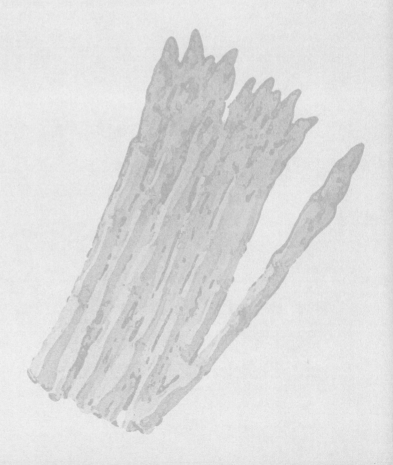

Cream of Oat Bran

Thick and rich, a bowl of this creamy cereal is like old-fashioned cream of wheat and provides 8 grams of protein. Walnuts and ground flaxseeds add more fiber and healthful omega-3 fats.

15 minutes 30 minutes 45 minutes

½ cup plain soymilk

¼ cup cold water

¼ cup oat bran

Pinch salt

Dash ground cinnamon

2 tablespoons chopped walnuts, optional

1 tablespoon ground flaxseeds, optional

Combine soymilk, water, oat bran and salt in microwave-proof bowl. Cook in microwave on high power for 3 minutes, or until mixture thickens to desired consistency, stopping and stirring after each minute. Top with cinnamon, and walnuts and flaxseeds, if using.

Per Serving: 120 cal; 8g prot; 4g total fat (0.5g sat. fat); 15g carb; 0mg chol; 15mg sod; 5g fiber; 1g sugars

Blueberry-Hazelnut Muffins

MAKES 12 MUFFINS

Skip the sugar high of coffee-shop goodies. These fiber- and protein-rich treats will keep you going till lunchtime.

15 minutes 30 minutes **45 minutes**

1 cup whole wheat pastry flour

1 cup sugar

¾ cup unbleached all-purpose flour

¼ cup wheat germ

2 teaspoons baking powder

2 teaspoons lemon zest

Pinch ground nutmeg

¾ cup low-fat sour cream

¼ cup low-fat milk

2 large eggs

2 tablespoons olive oil

1 cup fresh or frozen blueberries

½ cup chopped blanched or toasted hazelnuts

Nonstick cooking spray

1 Preheat oven to 350°F. Combine pastry flour, sugar, all-purpose flour, wheat germ, baking powder, lemon zest and nutmeg in medium-sized bowl.

2 Whisk together sour cream, milk and eggs in large bowl. Stir flour mixture into sour cream mixture. Add olive oil, and mix to combine. Fold in blueberries and hazelnuts.

3 Coat 12 muffin molds with nonstick cooking spray, or line muffin molds with paper cups. Scoop ½ cup batter into each mold.

4 Bake 25 minutes, or until toothpick inserted in center of one muffin comes out clean. Transfer to wire rack to cool. Serve warm or at room temperature.

Per Muffin: 229 cal; 5g prot; 9g total fat (2g sat. fat); 34g carb; 41mg chol; 21mg sod; 3g fiber; 17g sugars

Asparagus Scones

MAKES 15 SCONES

Whether you whip up a batch for brunch or serve them for afternoon tea, these flavorful scones are a great way to use leftover steamed asparagus spears that are a little too limp to serve a second time. Feel free to replace the cheddar with your favorite grate-able cheese, such as Gruyère, Parmesan or smoked mozzarella.

15 minutes | **30** minutes | 45 minutes

12 ounces steamed asparagus

2 cups unbleached all-purpose flour

1 tablespoon sugar

1 tablespoon baking powder

½ teaspoon salt

4 tablespoons (½ stick) unsalted butter, margarine or shortening

¾ cup plus 2 tablespoons buttermilk or soymilk, divided

1 cup grated cheddar cheese or soy cheddar cheese

½ teaspoon cayenne

¼ teaspoon freshly ground black pepper

1 Preheat oven to 425°F.

2 Trim tips from asparagus and reserve, and chop stalks into ¼-inch pieces. Stir together flour, sugar, baking powder and salt in large bowl. Cut butter into small pieces. Using your fingers, rub butter into flour mixture until mixture resembles coarse meal. Stir in ¾ cup buttermilk. Fold in cheese, asparagus pieces (but not tips), cayenne and pepper.

3 Turn dough onto floured work surface, and knead 6 or 7 times. Shape dough into ½-inch-thick rectangle. Using sharp knife, cut rectangle lengthwise into three strips. Cut each strip into five triangles. Place triangles on greased baking sheet. Brush scones with remaining 2 Tbs. buttermilk, then press 2 or 3 asparagus tips into tops.

4 Bake 12 to 15 minutes, or until tops are golden brown. Transfer to a wire rack. Serve warm.

Per Scone: 130 cal; 4g prot; 5g total fat (3.5g sat. fat); 15g carb; 15mg chol; 240mg sod; <1g fiber; 2g sugars

Whole Wheat Waffles

SERVES 6   VEGAN

Waffles made with silken tofu instead of eggs have a crisp and light
texture. Instead of the usual butter and syrup, try warmed applesauce or
sautéed apples and a dollop of yogurt; for a savory topping, try ratatouille,
mushroom sauce or creamed spinach. Any leftover waffles can be frozen
and popped into a toaster to reheat.

15 minutes | 30 minutes | 45 minutes

2 cups whole wheat pastry flour

1 tablespoon baking powder

12.3 ounces firm silken tofu

2 tablespoons olive oil

1 tablespoon apple cider vinegar

Olive oil or nonstick cooking spray

1 Preheat waffle iron.

2 Mix flour and baking powder in large bowl.
Combine tofu, oil, vinegar and 1¾ cups water
in blender or food processor. Blend until
smooth. Add extra water if needed—batter
should be pourable.

3 Brush waffle iron with olive oil, or spray
with nonstick cooking spray. Cover bottom
waffle grid with batter, using a rubber spatula
to spread it evenly. Cook waffles until crisp and
lightly browned. Repeat till batter is gone. Keep
finished waffles warm in a low oven. Serve warm.

Per Serving: 200 cal; 9g prot; 6g total fat (1g sat. fat);
30g carb; 0mg chol; 300mg sod; 5g fiber; 1g sugars

Breakfast Blueberry Quesadillas

SERVES 4

You can have this breakfast ready in no time. Vary the dried fruit depending on the season—dried cranberries and dried tart cherries are fine substitutes for the blueberries.

15 minutes **30** minutes 45 minutes

1 cup part-skim ricotta cheese

One 3-ounce package dried blueberries

⅓ cup packed brown sugar

1 teaspoon lemon extract

Zest of 1 lemon

4 whole wheat flour tortillas

1 cup part-skim mozzarella cheese

Nonstick cooking spray

4 tablespoons plain nonfat yogurt, for garnish

½ pint fresh blueberries, for garnish

1 Put ricotta cheese, blueberries, brown sugar, lemon extract and lemon zest in medium-sized bowl, and blend well.

2 Sprinkle one tortilla with ¼ cup mozzarella cheese. Put about ⅓ cup blueberry mixture on half of tortilla, and fold other half over it to enclose filling. Repeat with remaining tortillas, mozzarella and blueberry mixture.

3 Spray large skillet with nonstick cooking spray, and heat over medium heat. Cook quesadillas, two at a time, until golden on bottom, about 3 minutes. Flip over, and cook second side until golden. Top each quesadilla with 1 tablespoon yogurt and sprinkling of blueberries. Serve hot.

Per Serving: 490 cal; 20g prot; 14g total fat (7g sat. fat); 69g carb; 35mg chol; 420mg sod; 5g fiber; 33g sugars

Hearty Sweet Potato Hash

SERVES 6

This hearty hash is just too good to eat only in the morning. People love breakfast for dinner, so go ahead and switch the hash around—it works well either way.

15 minutes **30 minutes** 45 minutes

3 tablespoons vegetable oil, divided

1 large sweet potato, peeled and cubed

1 large yellow onion, peeled and diced (about 2 cups)

1 cup fresh or frozen corn kernels

3 cloves garlic, minced (1 tablespoon)

6 ounces soy "meat" crumbles

6 large eggs, beaten

Salt to taste

Freshly ground black pepper to taste

1 cup chopped fresh parsley, for garnish

1 Heat 2 tablespoons oil in large skillet over medium heat. Add sweet potato and onion, and sauté 10 minutes, or until vegetables are softened. Reduce heat to medium, add corn and garlic, and sauté mixture 2 minutes more.

2 Add remaining 1 tablespoon oil, and stir in soy "meat." Stir in eggs, and season with salt and pepper to taste. Cook 5 minutes, or until eggs are cooked through, stirring constantly. Remove from heat, spoon hash onto individual plates and garnish each serving with generous sprinkling of parsley.

Per Serving: 258 cal; 14g prot; 13g total fat (2g sat. fat); 23g carb; 212mg chol; 381mg sod; 4g fiber; 2g sugars

Skillet Potatoes with Soy "Sausage"

SERVES 4   VEGAN

Make this with leftover baked potatoes.

15 minutes 30 minutes **45** minutes

2 tablespoons olive oil

8 ounces frozen soy "sausage" links

1½ cups chopped yellow onion

2 medium-sized sweet potatoes,
    grated (5 cups)

2 medium-sized baked russet
    potatoes, diced (4 cups)

Salt to taste

Freshly ground black pepper to taste

1 In 10-inch nonstick skillet, heat 1 tablespoon oil over medium heat. Add soy "sausages," and cook, turning often, about 5 minutes. Remove to cutting board. Wipe out skillet. Heat remaining 1 tablespoon oil over medium heat. Add onion; cook, stirring often, about 7 minutes, or until soft. Meanwhile, cut "sausages" into bite-size pieces.

2 Add sweet potatoes to skillet. Cover and cook, stirring occasionally, 4 to 5 minutes, or until tender.

3 Add russet potatoes and "sausage" pieces to skillet. Season to taste with salt and black pepper, and mix well. Press mixture down lightly with a spatula. Cook until bottom is golden brown, 10 to 12 minutes. Serve hot.

Per Serving: 320 cal; 14g prot; 11g total fat
(1g sat. fat); 41g carb; 0mg chol; 290mg sod; 6g fiber;
8g sugars

Cheese Beignets

SERVES 8

Beignets are commonly referred to as the "Southerner's doughnut." In this family recipe, the dough should be stiff—add just enough water so that you can press the dough flat. To make cutting the stiff dough easier, use a floured pizza cutter.

15 minutes 30 minutes **45** minutes

2 cups unbleached all-purpose flour

½ cup finely minced fresh sage

1½ teaspoons baking powder

½ teaspoon salt

2 large eggs, lightly beaten

1 tablespoon olive oil

½ to 1 teaspoon hot sauce,
    to your taste

½ cup grated hard cheese, such as
    Parmesan or pecorino

Vegetable oil for frying

Coarse salt, for sprinkling

Cayenne or smoked paprika,
    for dusting

1 Stir together flour, sage, baking powder and salt in medium-sized bowl.

2 Whisk together eggs, olive oil and hot sauce in large bowl. Gradually stir in flour mixture. Add ¾ cup water a little at a time, combining well until dough is thick. Fold in cheese.

3 Press dough into ½-inch-thick rectangle on well-floured work surface. Cut into 1 ½-inch squares.

4 Pour vegetable oil into large skillet to depth of ½ inch, and heat over medium heat until small piece of dough sizzles gently in oil. (The dough should not brown immediately.)

5 Place beignet squares in oil, taking care not to overcrowd (you may need to fry in batches). Fry 3 minutes on each side, or until browned and done throughout. Remove with a slotted spoon to paper towels to drain. Sprinkle immediately with coarse salt. Right before serving, dust with cayenne.

Per Serving: 190 cal; 7g prot; 7g total fat (1.5g sat. fat); 25g carb; 55mg chol; 330mg sod; <1g fiber; 1g sugars

Breakfast Pizza

You'll get rave reviews about this made-for-mornings pizza.

15 minutes   30 minutes   **45** minutes

Nonstick cooking spray

One 8-ounce can low-fat refrigerated crescent dinner roll dough

7 ounces soy breakfast "sausage" patties

1 cup frozen shredded hash brown potatoes, thawed

1 cup shredded low-fat cheddar cheese

One 8-ounce carton egg substitute, or 4 large eggs

¼ cup skim milk or soymilk

2 teaspoons chopped fresh sage, or 1 tablespoon dried rubbed sage

½ teaspoon salt

¼ teaspoon crushed red pepper

1 Preheat oven to 375°F. Coat 12-inch pizza pan with nonstick cooking spray. Separate dough into triangles, and press triangles together to form single round crust. Crimp edges of dough with your fingers to form rim.

2 Heat a skillet over medium heat and cook "sausages" 5 to 7 minutes, breaking them into small crumbles. Drain on paper towels, and let cool slightly.

3 Top prepared dough with "sausage," potatoes and cheese. Whisk together egg substitute, milk, sage, salt and red pepper in medium-sized bowl. Carefully pour egg mixture over "sausage" mixture.

4 Bake 25 minutes, or until crust is browned. Cut into wedges, and serve warm.

3 1833 05523 0277

Per Serving: 219 cal; 16g prot; 8g total fat (2g sat. fat); 20g carb; 2mg chol; 720mg sod; 2g fiber; 3g sugars

Chilaquiles with Beans

SERVES 6

This offbeat version of a traditional Mexican dish should wake you up, especially when served with cinnamon-infused Mexican hot chocolate. But don't limit it to just breakfast. Served with guacamole, sour cream and chilled Mexican beer, the chilaquiles turn supper into a mini fiesta. Offer warmed corn or flour tortillas to mop up extra beans.

15 minutes **30 minutes** 45 minutes

Nonstick cooking spray

2 cups crushed tortilla chips, preferably lime-flavored, divided

4 plum tomatoes, coarsely chopped

One 4-ounce can diced green chiles

¾ cup tomatillo salsa

1 jalapeño chile, minced, optional

1 cup shredded part-skim mozzarella cheese

1 cup shredded low-fat or regular cheddar cheese

Two 15-ounce cans kidney beans, drained and rinsed

3 hard-boiled large eggs, thinly sliced, for garnish

½ cup chopped fresh cilantro, for garnish

1 bunch (4 ounces) green onions, thinly sliced, for garnish

1 Preheat oven to 450°F. Spray 2- to 3-quart baking dish with nonstick cooking spray. Line bottom of dish with 1 cup chips.

2 Heat medium-sized skillet over medium-high heat; cook tomatoes, green chiles, tomatillo salsa and jalapeño, if using, 5 to 7 minutes. Toss mozzarella and cheddar cheeses together in large bowl.

3 Spoon half of tomato mixture over chips. Layer 1 cup cheese and all beans over top. Top with remaining chips, tomato mixture and cheese. Cover dish with aluminum foil.

4 Bake about 15 minutes, or until cheese melts. Garnish with eggs, cilantro and green onions. Serve hot.

Per Serving: 360 cal; 24g prot; 11g total fat (3.5g sat. fat); 42g carb; 115mg chol; 750mg sod; 8g fiber; 5g sugars

Asparagus Goldenrod

SERVES 6

This is an early spring favorite, especially when made with eggs from free-range chickens.

1 pound fresh asparagus, ends trimmed

2 tablespoons (¼ stick) unsalted butter

2 tablespoons unbleached all-purpose flour

½ teaspoon salt

Pinch freshly ground black pepper

1 cup low-fat milk

3 hard-boiled large eggs

1 tablespoon fresh tarragon, or 1 teaspoon dried crushed tarragon

6 slices toast, cut in half diagonally

1 tablespoon snipped fresh chives, for garnish, optional

1 Bring large pot of salted water to a boil. Put asparagus in water and let water return to a boil. Remove pot from heat, and let asparagus stand 1 minute, or until crisp-tender. Drain, and cut spears diagonally into 2- to 3-inch pieces, reserving tips for garnish.

2 Melt butter in small saucepan over medium heat. Stir in flour, salt and pepper, and cook 30 seconds. Pour in milk, and cook, stirring constantly, until sauce thickens. Remove from heat.

3 Peel eggs, and remove yolks. Chop whites, reserving yolks for garnish. Stir egg whites and tarragon into white sauce. Arrange 2 toast points on each plate. Separate asparagus pieces into 6 equal portions, and place on toast. Top with white sauce. Press half of a cooked yolk through sieve to garnish each serving. Top with reserved asparagus tips and chopped chives, if using.

Per Serving: 230 cal; 9g prot; 8g total fat (3.5g sat. fat); 29g carb; 120mg chol; 420mg sod; 2g fiber; 5g sugars

2

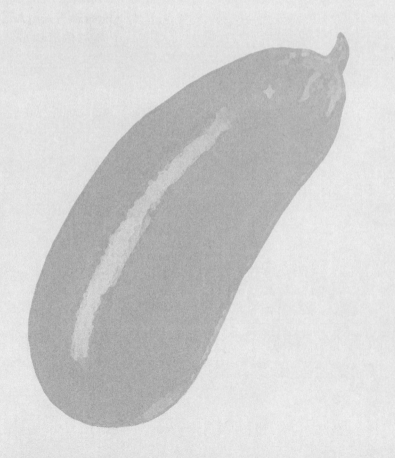

Lunch

Curried Tofu Scramble

SERVES 4   VEGAN

Adding curry powder, carrots and green onions to tofu makes it truly satisfying.

1 pound firm tofu, drained and cut into 16 cubes

2 tablespoons vegetable oil

3 cups grated carrots (about 4 medium-sized)

1 tablespoon curry powder

Salt to taste

½ cup chopped green onions, white and pale green parts only

1 Squeeze tofu gently but firmly, working with one cube of tofu at a time over sink, until it crumbles slightly and water drips out. Put in bowl.

2 Heat oil in large skillet over medium heat. Add carrots, and cook, stirring often, 5 minutes, or until tender.

3 Stir in curry powder, and cook, stirring, 1 minute. Add tofu, sprinkle with salt to taste, and cook, stirring, 3 minutes, or until tofu is evenly golden and firm. Add green onions, and cook, stirring often, about 1 minute. Serve hot.

Per Serving: 270 cal; 19g prot; 17g total fat (2g sat. fat); 15g carb; 0mg chol; 360mg sod; 6g fiber; 4g sugars

Super-Simple Tropical Couscous

SERVES 6   VEGAN

Turn couscous tropical with the medley of dried island fruit sold at most
supermarkets. If you prefer, you can concoct your own mixture using
tropical fruits such as dried papayas, mangoes and shredded coconut.

15 minutes 30 minutes 45 minutes

1 tablespoon vegetable oil

1½ cups uncooked couscous

One 6-ounce package dried tropical
   fruit medley

1 cup salted cashews

¼ cup plus 2 tablespoons mango
   chutney, or to taste

Bring 2 cups water along with oil to a boil in
medium-sized saucepan, and stir in couscous.
Bring back to a boil, cover and turn off heat. Let
stand until water is absorbed, 5 to 10 minutes.
Remove from heat, and stir in fruit, cashews and
chutney. Serve hot, warm or cold—your choice!

Per Serving: 450 cal; 10g prot; 13g total fat
(2.5g sat. fat); 73g carb; 0mg chol; 105mg sod;
5g fiber; 29g sugars

Vegetarian *Bahn Mi* with Pickled Carrots and Smoked Tofu

SERVES 4   VEGAN

Bahn mi are Vietnamese sandwiches that are typically filled with pickled vegetables and grilled meats. Substitute smoked tofu for the meat, and add a green onion aïoli for more flavor. The pickles can be made a day ahead.

PICKLES

2 medium-sized carrots, peeled and shredded

½ cup daikon radish (4 ounces), peeled and shredded

⅓ cup sugar

1 teaspoon salt

½ cup white vinegar

SANDWICH

2 tablespoons vegan mayonnaise

2 green onions, thinly sliced

Salt to taste

Freshly ground black pepper to taste

One 15-ounce French baguette, sliced in half lengthwise

6 ounces smoked tofu, cut into ¼-inch slices

½ English cucumber, thinly sliced (about 1 cup)

¼ cup fresh cilantro leaves

1 jalapeño chile, thinly sliced, optional

1 *To make Pickles:* Put carrots and daikon in small bowl, and add ½ teaspoon sugar and ½ teaspoon salt. Massage lightly for 1 minute. Rinse with water, and drain well. Wrap in paper towel, and squeeze out excess liquid. Put drained vegetables, vinegar and remaining sugar and salt into medium-sized bowl, and set aside.

2 *To make Sandwich:* Put vegan mayonnaise and green onions in small bowl, and stir to combine. Season to taste with salt and pepper.

3 Lay baguette on counter, and remove some soft inner bread. Spread bottom half with mayonnaise. Layer tofu on mayonnaise, followed by cucumber slices. Sprinkle cilantro and jalapeño slices over cucumbers.

4 Squeeze pickling liquid from carrot mixture, and layer on top of cilantro. Place top of baguette on top of sandwich, and press down firmly. Slice into 4 sections, and serve.

Per Serving: 285 cal; 13g prot; 6.5g total fat (1g sat. fat); 44g carb; 0mg chol; 962mg sod; 4g fiber; 9g sugars

Grilled American Sandwich

SERVES 4

Inspired by the beloved Monte Cristo—a French toast sandwich typically filled with a savory combination of ham, turkey or chicken and melted cheese—our unusual version merits applause. The addition of strawberry jam may sound odd, but trust us: The effect is delicious.

15 minutes **30 minutes** 45 minutes

3 large eggs

½ cup skim milk

2 teaspoons pure vanilla extract

4 slices whole wheat bread

Nonstick cooking spray

Four 2-ounce slices soy "sausage" roll

4 slices vegan Swiss or cheddar cheese

4 tablespoons strawberry jam

4 or more large strawberries, sliced, for garnish

Confectioners' sugar, for sprinkling

1 Beat together eggs, milk and vanilla extract in large baking pan. Soak bread in egg mixture 5 minutes, turning several times to ensure even absorption.

2 Meanwhile, spray large or electric skillet with nonstick cooking spray, press "sausage" slices flat and cook in skillet 2 minutes; turn, and brown second side. Remove from skillet, and set aside.

3 Re-spray skillet, and cook all bread on one side over medium heat. Turn bread, and layer one "sausage" slice, cheese slice and remaining "sausage" slice on cooked sides of two slices bread. Top filling with remaining slices bread, making a sandwich with uncooked sides facing out. Brown bottom slices, and, using spatula, turn sandwiches over to brown top slices. Press down on sandwiches with spatula, and when bottoms are golden, turn again and cook 2 minutes more, or until cheese begins to melt.

4 Put sandwiches on plates, and top each with 1 tablespoon strawberry jam and 1 sliced strawberry. Sprinkle with confectioners' sugar. Serve warm.

Per Serving: 310 cal; 20g prot; 10g total fat (1.5g sat. fat); 36g carb; 160mg chol; 680mg sod; 4g fiber; 20g sugars

Grilled Smoked Mozzarella Sandwiches

SERVES 2

The George Foreman grill does a great job of making toasted panini-like sandwiches with characteristic grill marks, without using butter or oil.

15 minutes 30 minutes 45 minutes

3 to 4 slices smoked mozzarella cheese

4 slices whole wheat bread

4 to 6 oil-packed sun-dried tomato halves

4 to 6 fresh basil leaves

1 Preheat grill to 300°F. (This will take about 5 minutes.)

2 Arrange mozzarella slices over 2 bread slices. Lay sun-dried tomato halves and basil leaves on cheese. Top with remaining bread slices, and cut sandwiches in half.

3 Place sandwiches on heated grill, and close top. Grill 2 to 3 minutes, or until bread is toasted and cheese is slightly melted. Serve hot.

Per Serving: 207 cal; 9g prot; 9g total fat (4.5g sat. fat); 23g carb; 22mg chol; 412mg sod; 3g fiber; 0g sugars

Grilled Cheese with Fig and Basil

SERVES 4

Fresh basil and fig preserves transform good ol' grilled cheese into a sophisticated sandwich. Honey lovers will like this recipe as is; others may prefer the less sweet honey-free version.

4 ounces chèvre (soft goat cheese)

1 tablespoon honey, optional

8 thin slices cinnamon-raisin bread

2 teaspoons minced fresh basil

2 tablespoons fig preserves

Nonstick cooking spray

1 Combine chèvre and honey, if using, in bowl, and mix until well blended. Spread about 1 tablespoon mixture on each of 4 bread slices; top each with ½ teaspoon basil. Spread remaining slices of bread with 1½ teaspoons fig preserves. Close sandwiches, and lightly coat both sides with nonstick cooking spray.

2 Heat large nonstick skillet over medium heat. Add 2 sandwiches to skillet. Place heavy skillet or pot on top of sandwiches, and press gently to flatten. Cook 3 minutes on each side, or until bread is lightly toasted (leave skillet or pot on sandwiches while they cook). Repeat with remaining sandwiches. Serve warm.

Per Serving: 280 cal; 10g prot; 10g total fat (5g sat. fat); 40g carb; 30mg chol; 320mg sod; 3g fiber; 20g sugars

Chickpea and Eggplant Pita Pockets

Cumin and mint complement succulent eggplant and chickpeas in these stuffed pita pockets.

Six 4-inch pita breads

2 tablespoons olive oil

1 pound Japanese eggplant, unpeeled, cut into ¾-inch cubes

1¼ cups chopped sweet onions, preferably Vidalia

One 15.5-ounce can chickpeas, drained and rinsed, ½ cup bean liquid reserved

1 tablespoon fresh lemon juice

2 teaspoons ground cumin

3 tablespoons minced fresh mint

Salt to taste

Freshly ground black pepper to taste

1 Preheat oven to 350°F.

2 Stack pitas in aluminum foil, and wrap. Bake until heated through, about 10 minutes.

3 Meanwhile, heat oil in large nonstick skillet over medium-high heat. Add eggplant and onions, and cook, stirring often, until softened and beginning to brown, about 10 minutes. Add chickpeas, lemon juice and cumin, and cook, stirring occasionally, about 5 minutes, or until heated through. If mixture seems dry, add enough chickpea liquid to moisten. Stir in mint. Season to taste with salt and pepper.

4 Remove pitas from oven, and fill with eggplant mixture. Serve warm.

Per Serving: 224 cal; 11g prot; 6.5g total fat (1g sat. fat); 58g carb; 0mg chol; 541mg sod; 8g fiber; 7g sugars

Seville Burgers with Olive-Orange Relish

SERVES 8

Contest winner A trip to Spain inspired Kevin West to come up with these savory patties. If the burgers don't hold together well—various brands of whole-grain bread tested differently—simply process another piece of bread into crumbs, and fold them into the mixture. This recipe was the second-place winner in the 2005 *Vegetarian Times* Recipe Contest.

15 minutes **30 minutes** 45 minutes

OLIVE-ORANGE RELISH

½ cup chopped pimiento-stuffed green olives

3 tablespoons orange marmalade

SEVILLE BURGERS

3 large slices whole-grain bread

One 15-ounce can light kidney beans, drained and rinsed

1 cup chunky-style salsa

½ cup chopped green onions

1 tablespoon fresh lemon juice

2½ teaspoons dried oregano leaves

2 cloves garlic, minced (2 teaspoons)

2 teaspoons cornstarch

½ teaspoon salt

1 large egg

1 cup shredded manchego cheese

3 tablespoons olive oil

8 whole-grain burger buns, split

1 cup fresh baby spinach leaves, rinsed and dried

1 *To make Olive-Orange Relish:* Stir olives and marmalade together in small bowl. Set aside.

2 *To make Seville Burgers:* Blend bread into crumbs in food processor. Transfer to large bowl.

3 Pulse beans, salsa, green onions, lemon juice, oregano, garlic, cornstarch, salt and egg 5 times in food processor, or until blended but chunky. Add bean mixture and cheese to breadcrumbs and mix well. Shape into 8 patties.

4 Heat oil in large nonstick skillet over medium heat. Cook patties 5 minutes on each side, or until browned.

5 Place burgers on bottom halves of buns. Add relish, spinach leaves and top halves of buns, and serve.

Per Serving: 256 cal; 10g prot; 11g total fat (3g sat. fat); 30g carb; 37mg chol; 800mg sod; 8g fiber; 3g sugars

Spinach-Tempeh Quesadillas

SERVES 6 VEGAN

If you like things spicy, you can kick up the heat in this recipe by using a picante salsa and adding some chopped jalapeños to the mixture. If you use a large skillet or griddle, you can cook more than 2 quesadillas at a time. Offer scoops of guacamole served on leaf lettuce as a side dish, and pass fresh fruit with cookies for dessert.

1 tablespoon vegetable oil

8 ounces tempeh, cubed

2 tomatillos, diced

1 pound fresh spinach leaves, stems trimmed, rinsed and dried

2 cups salsa, divided

Six 8- or 9-inch whole wheat tortillas

One 7-ounce package shredded soy cheddar cheese

Nonstick cooking spray

1 Heat oil in large skillet, and sauté cubed tempeh and tomatillos for 5 to 8 minutes.

2 Meanwhile, put freshly washed spinach into large saucepan, leaving rinse water on leaves. Cover pot, and steam over medium heat until spinach is completely wilted, about 5 minutes.

3 Preheat broiler.

4 Stir 1 cup salsa into tempeh mixture, and continue cooking until heated through, about 2 minutes. Put 1 tortilla flat on work surface, and scoop about ⅓ cup tempeh filling over half of tortilla. Sprinkle with about 2 tablespoons soy cheese; fold top over filling. Repeat with remaining tempeh mixture until all tortillas are filled.

5 Spray large nonstick skillet with cooking spray, and heat over medium heat. Add folded tortillas (as many as will fit comfortably in pan), and cook until cheese melts and both sides turn golden brown, 4 to 5 minutes total. Repeat until all quesadillas have been browned.

6 When finished, put quesadillas in large baking pan. Top quesadillas with remaining salsa and cheese, and broil until cheese melts. Serve hot.

Per Serving: 330 cal; 20g prot; 11g total fat (0.5g sat. fat); 34g carb; 0mg chol; 650mg sod; 6g fiber; 3g sugars

Chipotle Black Bean Tacos with Roasted Butternut Squash

SERVES 5

These tacos were inspired by the tacos served at the Border Grill in Santa Monica, California. The sweetness of the butternut squash pairs perfectly with the pickled onions and the earthy black beans. You can often find peeled and chopped butternut squash in the produce section.

15 minutes | **30 minutes** | 45 minutes

PICKLES

1 cup red wine vinegar

½ cup light brown sugar

½ teaspoon salt

1 cup thinly sliced red onion

TACOS

12 ounces butternut squash, cut into ½-inch cubes (about 2 cups)

3 tablespoons canola oil, divided

Salt to taste

Freshly ground black pepper to taste

¼ cup chopped fresh cilantro

½ teaspoon cumin seeds

Two 15-ounce cans black beans, drained and rinsed

2 chipotle chiles in adobo, finely chopped (about 2 tablespoons)

2 cloves garlic, minced (2 teaspoons)

1 teaspoon light brown sugar

1 teaspoon balsamic vinegar

Corn tortillas

Queso fresco

Per Serving: 371 cal; 12g prot; 10.5g total fat (1g sat. fat); 65g carb; 0mg chol; 426mg sod; 13g fiber; 10g sugars

1 *To make Pickles:* Put vinegar, sugar and salt in medium bowl, and stir until sugar dissolves. Add onion; stir to combine, and set aside.

2 *To make Tacos:* Preheat oven to 375°F.

3 Toss butternut squash in medium bowl with 2 tablespoons oil and salt and pepper to taste. Transfer squash to greased sheet pan, and bake 15 to 20 minutes, stirring occasionally, until squash is caramelized and tender. Put squash in small bowl, and toss with cilantro.

4 Heat remaining 1 tablespoon oil in medium saucepan over medium heat. Add cumin seeds, and stir for 1 minute, or until they start to sputter. Add beans, chipotles, garlic, brown sugar and 1 cup water. Bring to a simmer, and stir with wooden spoon, smashing beans against side of saucepan to mash them. Simmer 5 to 7 minutes, and then add vinegar and salt and pepper to taste. Remove from heat.

5 To serve, warm the tortillas, and place them and taco components, including *queso fresco,* on table; have diners assemble tacos as they eat.

Hot and Heart-y Valentine Sandwiches

Here's a heart- and hand-warming sandwich for a special winter lunch. Hot lemon tea and salad with vinaigrette add a tangy touch. How about a heart-shaped chocolate cake for dessert?

15 minutes **30 minutes** 45 minutes

2 mini baguettes, about 5 ounces each

1 cup quartered artichoke hearts, well drained

4 pieces hearts of palm, chopped

½ red bell pepper, diced

3 tablespoons shredded low-fat mozzarella cheese

2 tablespoons soy mayonnaise

2 tablespoons grated Parmesan cheese

1 teaspoon dried onion flakes

Salt to taste

Freshly ground black pepper to taste

1 Preheat oven to 425°F.

2 Slice tops off baguettes about ¼ inch down. Scoop out centers, and save for making bread-crumbs. Set baguettes aside, each on a piece of aluminum foil, ready for wrapping.

3 Combine all the remaining ingredients in large bowl, and stir together to mix well. Spoon equal amounts of mixture into each baguette, put baguette tops on filling and wrap tightly in foil.

4 Bake about 10 minutes, or until cheese melts and baguettes are heated through. Unwrap, and serve hot.

Per Serving: 370 cal; 11g prot; 11g total fat (2.5g sat. fat); 59g carb; 5mg chol; 750mg sod; 5g fiber; 1g sugars

All-Day Burrito

SERVES 1

An egg pancake replaces the tortilla in this breakfast or lunch dish.

15 minutes 30 minutes 45 minutes

2 tablespoons medium or mild salsa

1 large egg, plus 2 large egg whites

1 tablespoon chopped fresh cilantro

Freshly ground black pepper to taste

Nonstick cooking spray

1 strip soy "bacon"

¼ cup shredded soy Monterey Jack or cheddar cheese

1 Drain salsa in fine-mesh strainer; set aside.

2 Whisk together egg, egg whites and cilantro in small bowl. Season with black pepper, and set aside.

3 Coat 8-inch skillet with nonstick cooking spray, and heat over medium-high heat. Cook soy "bacon" 2 minutes, turning once. Set aside; wipe out pan.

4 Re-spray pan, and heat over medium heat. Pour in egg mixture; as it begins to set, lift and tilt pan, lifting cooked edges and letting liquid part run underneath. When almost completely set, sprinkle soy cheese over the top. Cook about 2 minutes, or until cheese is melted. Slide pancake onto plate. Place "bacon" strip down center. Spoon salsa on "bacon." Fold over sides of pancake. Serve immediately, or let cool and serve at room temperature.

Per Serving: 210 cal; 23g prot; 9g total fat (1.5g sat. fat); 7g carb; 215mg chol; 880mg sod; 0g fiber; 3g sugars

Spicy Sloppy Joes

SERVES 6   VEGAN

Ale adds a subtle richness to this updated version of the classic chili hash. Mound the Sloppy Joe filling on soft sandwich rolls, and top with sliced avocados and shredded lettuce. You can easily double this recipe for a party.

15 minutes **30 minutes** 45 minutes

3 tablespoons canola oil

1 large green bell pepper, chopped

4 large cloves garlic, minced (4 teaspoons)

1½ pounds soy "meat" crumbles

3 tablespoons chili powder

1¼ cups pale ale or brown ale, at room temperature

¾ cup low-sodium bottled chili sauce

2 tablespoons low-sodium soy sauce

1 to 2 jalapeño chiles, diced

1 cup finely chopped green onions

Salt to taste

Freshly ground black pepper to taste

1 Warm oil in large heavy pot over medium-high heat. Add green pepper and garlic, and sauté, stirring frequently, 5 minutes.

2 Stir in soy "meat" crumbles and chili powder. Cook 1 to 2 minutes, until fragrant.

3 Add ale, chili sauce, soy sauce and jalapeños; mix well. Reduce heat to medium-low, and simmer, stirring often, about 15 minutes, until thickened.

4 Mix in green onions, and season with salt and pepper to taste. Serve warm.

Per ⅔ **Cup Sloppy Joe Mixture:** 285 cal; 24g prot; 17g total fat (2g sat. fat); 32g carb; 0mg chol; 828mg sod; 9g fiber; 11g sugars

Curry and Chickpea Lettuce Wraps

SERVES 2   VEGAN

Curry paste (available in the Asian foods section of most supermarkets) is a thick, spicy seasoning used in Indian curries and stews. For a fast flavor lift, stir 1 teaspoon into canned soups or bottled salad dressings.

15 minutes 30 minutes 45 minutes

2 tablespoons prepared curry paste

4 ounces soy "meat" crumbles

2 cups fresh baby spinach leaves, rinsed and dried

½ cup shredded carrots

½ cup diced tomatoes

½ cup chickpeas (from 15.5-ounce can), drained and rinsed

6 large lettuce leaves, rinsed and dried

1 Whisk curry paste into ⅓ cup water in large microwave-safe bowl. Add all the remaining ingredients except lettuce leaves. Cover, and microwave on high 3 minutes.

2 Stir mixture to combine; cover and cook on high 2 minutes more, or until vegetables are tender.

3 Spoon about ⅓ cup curry mixture onto each lettuce leaf. Wrap leaf around mixture, and eat with your fingers.

Per Serving: 231 cal; 18g prot; 7.5g total fat (1.5g sat. fat); 24g carb; 0mg chol; 554mg sod; 11g fiber; 7g sugars

Greek Salad Pitas

SERVES 6

To pack this for lunch, wrap the pita pockets separately, and fill them with the salad just before serving. Or enjoy the chopped salad on its own with a bowl of soup for dinner. Pepperoncini are small, thin pickled chile peppers that range in spiciness from medium to medium-hot. Look for them in the Italian section of large supermarkets.

15 minutes 30 minutes 45 minutes

1 cup peeled, seeded and diced cucumber

1 cup diced red bell pepper

1 cup diced zucchini

⅓ cup crumbled feta cheese

¼ cup diced red onion

¼ cup chopped pepperoncini, optional

¼ cup chopped black olives, preferably kalamata

2 tablespoons extra virgin olive oil

1 tablespoon fresh lemon juice

1 teaspoon red wine vinegar

1 teaspoon dried oregano

Salt to taste

Freshly ground black pepper to taste

Three 6-inch whole wheat pita breads, cut in half

6 curly-leaf lettuce leaves, rinsed and dried

1 Combine cucumber, bell pepper, zucchini, feta, onion, pepperoncini, olives, oil, lemon juice, vinegar and oregano in large bowl, and toss to mix. Season to taste with salt and pepper.

2 Line each pita half with one lettuce leaf; fill with ½ cup salad mixture.

Per Serving: 210 cal; 6g prot; 9g total fat (2.5g sat. fat); 28g carb; 5mg chol; 410mg sod; 4g fiber; 3g sugars

Thai Rice Pancakes

SERVES 8 (MAKES SIXTEEN 4-INCH PANCAKES)

Why haul out a wok when you can get all the exotic flavors of Thai fried rice in these little pancakes? Make them with any kind of leftover rice, and serve them as a light lunch with a green salad dressed in a sesame-ginger vinaigrette—or for an appetizer, garnished with grated carrots or mango slices. Sriracha is a Southeast Asian hot chili sauce, available in the Asian foods section of many supermarkets.

15 minutes **30 minutes** 45 minutes

2 large eggs

¼ cup low-fat coconut milk

¼ cup chopped fresh cilantro

1 tablespoon minced peeled fresh ginger

2 cups cooked rice

1 bunch green onions, chopped (about 1 cup)

⅓ cup chopped unsalted peanuts

¼ cup unbleached all-purpose flour

⅛ teaspoon sriracha chili sauce or other hot sauce, optional

Salt to taste, optional

Freshly ground black pepper to taste, optional

Nonstick cooking spray

1 Whisk together eggs and coconut milk in large bowl. Stir in cilantro and ginger. Add rice, green onions, peanuts, flour and hot sauce, if using, and mix well. Season with salt and pepper, if using.

2 Coat large nonstick skillet with nonstick cooking spray and heat over medium heat. Drop ¼-cup dollops of batter into hot skillet. Smooth batter into flat rounds with spatula. Cook 4 to 5 minutes, or until bottoms are golden brown. Flip pancakes, and cook 3 to 4 minutes more, or until both sides are browned and crispy. Remove pancakes to warm plate, and repeat with remaining batter. Serve immediately.

Per Serving: 134 cal; 5g prot; 5.5g total fat (1g sat. fat); 16g carb; 53mg chol; 25mg sod; 1g fiber; 1g sugars

Sugar Snap Pea Summer Rolls

SERVES 8   VEGAN

Rice paper wrappers for these Vietnamese-style summer rolls can be found
in Asian grocery stores, as can the Indonesian *sambal oelek* hot sauce.

DIPPING SAUCE

¼ cup low-sodium soy sauce

¼ cup rice wine vinegar

¼ cup water

2 teaspoons dark sesame oil

1 teaspoon *sambal oelek*

SUMMER ROLLS

32 sugar snap peas (about 12 ounces)

1 carrot

8 green onions

One 8-ounce package rice vermicelli

2 tablespoons toasted sesame seeds

1 teaspoon fresh lime juice

½ teaspoon salt

¼ teaspoon freshly ground white
    pepper

8 rice paper wrappers

32 fresh mint leaves, plus extras

Per Serving: 190 cal; 6g prot; 2.5g total fat (0g sat.
fat); 35g carb; 0mg chol; 370mg sod; 2g fiber;
3g sugars

1 *To make Dipping Sauce:* Whisk all the ingredients together in small bowl. Set aside.

2 *To make Summer Rolls:* Bring pot of salted water to a boil. Cook snap peas 2 minutes. Drain, and immediately plunge into cold water. Peel carrot into about 40 long, thin strips. Wash and trim green onions to 3 inches long.

3 Put rice vermicelli in large bowl, and pour boiling water over to cover; let stand 3 minutes. Drain, and rinse with cold water. Return noodles to bowl, and stir in sesame seeds, lime juice, salt and pepper.

4 Place one rice paper wrapper on clean work surface. Dip clean dish towel in cold water, and moisten wrapper on both sides to soften, making sure to wet edges well. When soft, place 4 mint leaves in line down center. Top with ¼ cup noodle mixture, placing it in log shape and leaving about 1 inch of space on each side. Set 4 cooked sugar snap peas on top of noodles. Place green onion on top, and scatter with 4 or 5 carrot strips.

5 To close roll, gently lift top edge of rice paper wrapper from work surface, and roll it tightly once over filling. Carefully fold in both sides over filling, and roll wrapper toward you tightly to seal. Repeat with remaining wrappers and filling ingredients. If not eating immediately, chill well. Serve with dipping sauce and extra mint leaves.

Chilled Tofu Salad with Ginger, Green Onions, Asparagus and Sesame

SERVES 4   VEGAN

This is a great easy lunch for those summer days when you don't feel like cooking. The combination of cool, custardy tofu with a tart sesame vinaigrette makes for a refreshing lunch that won't weigh you down. Try to find the freshest silken tofu for this recipe.

15 minutes   30 minutes   45 minutes

VINAIGRETTE

4 tablespoons low-sodium soy sauce

3 tablespoons mirin

2 tablespoons seasoned rice vinegar

½ teaspoon dark sesame oil

¼ teaspoon chili oil

TOFU SALAD

12 ounces asparagus, trimmed

20 ounces silken tofu, drained and cut into eight 2-inch squares

2 green onions, minced (about ¼ cup)

2 teaspoons grated peeled fresh ginger

3 tablespoons toasted sesame seeds

1 *To make Vinaigrette:* Put all the ingredients in small bowl, and stir to combine. Set aside.

2 *To make Tofu Salad:* Put asparagus in microwave-safe dish with ¼ cup water, and cook on high 45 to 60 seconds, or until crisp-tender. Rinse asparagus under cold water, drain and wrap in paper towels to dry. Slice into ¼-inch coins. Distribute asparagus among 4 shallow bowls.

3 Center 2 pieces tofu on top of asparagus in each bowl. Place 1 tablespoon green onions and ½ teaspoon ginger in little mounds on tofu in each dish. Top with a generous sprinkling of sesame seeds. Pour 2 tablespoons vinaigrette around tofu in each bowl, and serve.

Per Serving: 185 cal; 10g prot; 8g total fat (0.5g sat. fat); 15g carb; 0mg chol; 759mg sod; 1g fiber; 10g sugars

Black Soybean Tabbouleh

SERVES 4   VEGAN

Canned black soybeans, high in protein and fiber, replace the traditional bulgur. Combining them with crunchy, high-fiber fresh veggies makes a perfect lunch.

15 minutes | **30 minutes** | 45 minutes

One 15-ounce can black soybeans, drained and rinsed

2 large plum tomatoes, seeded and chopped

1 medium-sized green bell pepper, chopped

1 packed cup chopped fresh Italian parsley leaves

Juice of 1 lemon

1 teaspoon salt

1/8 teaspoon cayenne, or to taste

1 tablespoon extra virgin olive oil

1 packed cup fresh mint leaves, cut into thin strips

1 Combine soybeans, tomatoes, green pepper and parsley in large bowl.

2 Whisk lemon juice with salt and cayenne in small bowl. Mix in oil. Pour over bean mixture; toss well. Mix in mint. Let sit 20 minutes to let flavors meld. Will keep tightly covered in refrigerator 24 hours.

Per Serving: 180 cal; 12g prot; 5g total fat (0.5g sat. fat); 20g carb; 0mg chol; 650mg sod; 10g fiber; 3g sugars

3

Appetizers

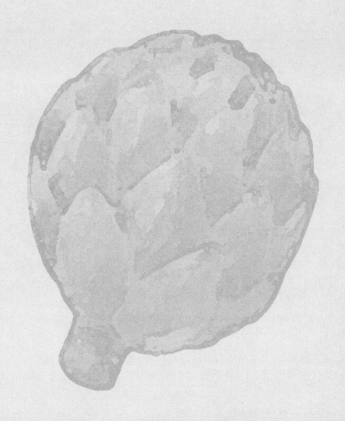

Edamame Hummus

SERVES 4   VEGAN

Using edamame (soybeans harvested while green to eat as a vegetable) instead of garbanzo beans gives this dip a fresh, sprightly flavor—and it doesn't need a drop of oil. Serve it as you would traditional hummus; it's delicious with pita bread. Or mound it onto a large plate, garnish with paprika and surround it with either cooked or raw veggies.

15 minutes 30 minutes 45 minutes

1½ cups frozen shelled edamame

½ cup fresh flat-leaf parsley leaves

3 tablespoons tahini

3 tablespoons fresh lemon juice

2 cloves garlic, chopped (2 teaspoons)

Salt to taste

1 Prepare edamame according to package directions, omitting salt. Drain.

2 Combine edamame, parsley, tahini, 3 tablespoons water, lemon juice, garlic and salt in food processor; blend 1 to 2 minutes, or until smooth. Spoon hummus into serving bowl and serve at room temperature.

Per Serving: 149 cal; 8g prot; 8g total fat (1g sat. fat); 11g carb; 0mg chol; 322mg sod; 4g fiber; 1g sugars

Hummus with "Ground Meat," Onions and Toasted Pine Nuts

SERVES 6   VEGAN

Here is a great appetizer for a party; this hummus only takes 15 to 20 minutes to prepare. It can be served with pita chips or an assortment of raw vegetables such as endive leaves, carrot sticks and radishes.

15 minutes 30 minutes 45 minutes

1 tablespoon olive oil

½ cup diced yellow onion

10 ounces soy "meat" crumbles

½ teaspoon ground allspice

½ teaspoon ground paprika

¼ teaspoon ground cinnamon

¼ teaspoon chili powder

2 tablespoons pine nuts, toasted

Salt to taste

Freshly ground black pepper to taste

One 16-ounce container prepared hummus

Olive oil, for drizzling

Whole wheat pitas or pita chips

1 Heat oil in large skillet over medium heat. Add onion, and sauté 5 to 7 minutes, or until translucent and starting to brown. Add soy "meat" crumbles, allspice, paprika, cinnamon and chili powder, and sauté 3 to 5 minutes. Remove from heat, and stir in pine nuts. Season to taste with salt and pepper.

2 Spoon hummus onto large round plate. Mound the "meat" mixture on top, leaving 1-inch hummus border around the outside. Drizzle with olive oil, and serve with pitas.

Per Serving: 231 cal; 14g prot; 11.5g total fat (1.5g sat. fat); 20g carb; 0mg chol; 487mg sod; 6g fiber; 2g sugars

Hot Artichoke Dip

MAKES ABOUT 2½ CUPS

Everyone loves spinach-artichoke dip, but it's typically a fat-and-calorie fiesta. Not this recipe—yet you'd never know it.

15 minutes 30 minutes 45 minutes

12 ounces light silken tofu

2 tablespoons reduced-fat mayonnaise

1 tablespoon Dijon mustard

1 tablespoon fresh lemon juice

2 cloves garlic, minced (2 teaspoons)

½ teaspoon onion powder

One 15.5-ounce can artichoke quarters in water, drained, rinsed and chopped

1 cup frozen chopped spinach, thawed and squeezed dry

½ cup grated Parmesan cheese

Ground paprika, for dusting

1 Preheat oven to 400°F. Purée tofu, mayonnaise, mustard, lemon juice, garlic and onion powder in blender or food processor until smooth. Transfer to medium-sized bowl.

2 Stir artichokes, spinach and cheese into tofu mixture. Spoon into 8-inch glass pie or casserole dish. Bake 20 minutes. Dust with paprika; serve hot.

Per Tablespoon: 16 cal; 1g prot; 1g total fat (0.5g sat. fat); 1g carb; 1mg chol; 56mg sod; <1g fiber; <1g sugars

Creamy Maple-Pumpkin Spread

You'll be surprised at how quickly this spread will disappear, especially if you serve it with sliced apples and pears.

15 minutes | 30 minutes | **45** minutes

¾ cup light cream cheese

½ cup canned pumpkin

⅓ cup packed light brown sugar

1 tablespoon maple syrup

1 teaspoon ground cinnamon

Combine cream cheese, pumpkin and brown sugar in electric mixer bowl; beat at medium speed until well blended. Add syrup and cinnamon, and beat until smooth. Cover, and chill 30 minutes before serving.

Per Tablespoon: 31 cal; 1g prot; 1g total fat (0.5g sat. fat); 4g carb; 3mg chol; 35mg sod; <1g fiber; 4g sugars

Muhammarah (Red Pepper and Walnut Spread)

SERVES 4   VEGAN

A popular dip throughout North Africa, *muhammarah* is a great alternative to hummus. Serve with pita triangles or thin rounds of French bread.

15 minutes | 30 minutes | 45 minutes

½ cup walnuts

2 red bell peppers, roasted and peeled

2 tablespoons dry breadcrumbs

2 tablespoons olive oil

2 tablespoons raspberry vinegar

1 teaspoon ground cumin

½ teaspoon cayenne

½ teaspoon freshly ground black pepper

¼ teaspoon salt, or more to taste

¼ cup chopped fresh parsley, optional

1 Heat medium-sized nonstick skillet over medium heat. Add walnuts, and cook 3 to 4 minutes, stirring often, or until browned and fragrant. Remove from pan, and let cool.

2 Put all of the ingredients except parsley in food processor. Purée until smooth. Spoon into small bowl. Sprinkle with parsley, if using. Serve at room temperature.

Per Serving: 100 cal; 2g prot; 8g total fat (1g sat. fat); 5g carb; 0mg chol; 88mg sod; 2g fiber; 0g sugars

Bruschetta with Red Pepper Purée

SERVES 6

Jarred roasted red peppers work beautifully here. You can make and chill the purée up to a day before serving. This recipe makes about 1½ cups purée.

`15 minutes` `30 minutes` `45 minutes`

12 bruschetta toasts (See recipe, right)

RED PEPPER PURÉE

One 16-ounce jar roasted, peeled, brine-packed red peppers, drained and rinsed

1 large clove garlic (1 teaspoon)

3 tablespoons soft unseasoned breadcrumbs

2 tablespoons sun-dried tomato pesto

2 tablespoons balsamic vinegar

Salt to taste

Freshly ground black pepper to taste

Extra virgin olive oil

1 Blot peppers with paper towels until dry.

2 Put garlic down feed tube of food processor with motor running, and process about 15 seconds, until finely chopped. Add peppers, breadcrumbs, pesto and vinegar, and purée until smooth. Season to taste with salt and pepper.

3 Spread 1 heaping tablespoon purée on each bruschetta toast, on side rubbed with garlic. Sprinkle with olive oil, and serve.

Bruschetta Toasts

MAKES 12 TOASTS

For an even more authentic taste of Tuscany, toast these on the grill.

Twelve ½-inch-thick slices good-quality Italian bread

1 large clove garlic, cut in half

1 Preheat broiler, and place oven rack about 6 inches from heat.

2 Place bread on baking sheet, and broil 2 to 4 minutes, or until crisp and golden. Turn toast over, and repeat. When cool enough to handle, rub one side of each toast with cut garlic clove.

Per Serving: 252 cal; 6g prot; 8.5g total fat (1.5g sat. fat); 36g carb; <1mg chol; 568mg sod; 2g fiber; 4g sugars

Tomato-Avocado Salsamole

MAKES 1 CUP   VEGAN

This recipe is a cross between guacamole and salsa—but lower in calories than the former and more healthful than the latter, thanks to avocado's anti-cancer/anti-cholesterol compounds. Like regular salsa, it's great as a dip or as a topping for burritos and tacos.

15 minutes | 30 minutes | 45 minutes

¼ cup finely chopped red onion

1 tablespoon fresh lime juice

1 tablespoon cider vinegar

1 teaspoon minced jalapeño chile,
    or more to taste

1 clove garlic, minced (1 teaspoon)

¼ teaspoon salt

1 ripe, peeled avocado, preferably
    Hass, pitted and coarsely mashed

1 medium-sized tomato, chopped

¼ cup chopped fresh cilantro

Combine onion, lime juice, vinegar, jalapeño, garlic and salt in small bowl. Add avocado, tomato and cilantro; stir well. Serve immediately.

Per 2 Tablespoons: 45 cal; 1g prot; 4g total fat
(0.5g sat. fat); 4g carb; 0mg chol; 75mg sod; 2g fiber;
1g sugars

Clementine Salsa

MAKES ABOUT 2 CUPS   VEGAN

People who love salsa will find this version irresistible. Try it with your favorite tortilla chips, on sandwiches or simply on a bed of crisp lettuce as a side salad. It's light, clean and exceptionally refreshing. Use cherry tomatoes if regular ones aren't in season.

15 minutes 30 minutes 45 minutes

3 clementines, peeled and chopped

2 cups chopped very ripe tomatoes (about 1¼ pounds)

¼ cup chopped white onion

6 tablespoons finely chopped fresh cilantro

1 tablespoon fresh lime juice, or more to taste

¼ teaspoon salt, or more to taste

Combine all ingredients in medium-sized bowl, and mix to blend. Taste for seasoning, adding more lime juice or salt if desired. Serve at room temperature or chilled; this salsa is even better the next day.

Per ¼ Cup: 25 cal; 1g prot; 0g total fat (0g sat. fat); 6g carb; 0mg chol; 80mg sod; 1g fiber; 4g sugars

Eggplant "Caviar"

MAKES ABOUT 3 CUPS   VEGAN

This spread may be made up to 2 days ahead and refrigerated. Bring it to room temperature, and serve with toasted bread slices.

15 minutes · **30** minutes · **45** minutes

2 tablespoons olive oil, divided

1 firm eggplant (about 1¼ pounds), cut into ½-inch cubes

1 medium-sized yellow onion, chopped

2 cloves garlic, minced (2 teaspoons)

Salt to taste

3 medium-sized ripe tomatoes (about 12 ounces), cut into ½-inch cubes

½ cup fresh basil leaves, chopped

¼ cup fresh flat-leaf parsley leaves, chopped

3 tablespoons fresh lemon juice

½ teaspoon sugar

Freshly ground black pepper to taste

1 Heat 1 tablespoon oil in large nonstick skillet over medium-high heat. Add eggplant, onion, garlic and salt to taste, and cook, stirring often, about 7 minutes, or until eggplant begins to brown. Reduce heat, cover and cook, stirring occasionally, about 10 minutes more, or until eggplant is tender. Transfer to large bowl, and let cool.

2 Add tomatoes, basil, parsley, lemon juice, sugar, remaining 1 tablespoon oil, and salt and pepper to taste. Blend well. Serve at room temperature.

Per Tablespoon: 11 cal; <1g prot; 0.5g total fat (0g sat. fat); 1g carb; 0mg chol; 13mg sod; <1g fiber; 1g sugars

Pumpkin Seeds with Garlic and Chile

MAKES ABOUT 2 CUPS   VEGAN

These pumpkin seeds are the perfect *botana* (cocktail snack) with Posada Punch (page 192)—spicy, salty and studded with bits of chewy, caramelized garlic.

| 15 minutes | **30** minutes | 45 minutes |

3 cups raw pumpkin seeds

3 tablespoons vegetable oil

2 heads garlic (about 24 cloves), cloves sliced

2 teaspoons ground chile de arbol powder or cayenne

1 teaspoon kosher or coarse sea salt

1 Preheat oven to 350°F.

2 Toast pumpkin seeds on ungreased baking sheet 10 minutes, or until light brown, shaking sheet occasionally so seeds cook evenly.

3 Meanwhile, heat oil in large skillet over medium-low heat. Add garlic, and cook 10 to 12 minutes, stirring often. As garlic slices begin to brown and caramelize, watch carefully to make sure they don't burn. Transfer to large bowl.

4 Add pumpkin seeds, chile powder and salt to garlic. Stir well to coat. Serve warm or at room temperature.

Per ¼ Cup Serving: 340 cal; 13g prot; 29g total fat (5g sat. fat); 12g carb; 0mg chol; 252mg sod; 2g fiber; <1g sugars

Super-Fast Fondue with Steamed Veggies

SERVES 4

Easy to double, this recipe is great for a group lunch, a small, quick dorm dinner party or entertaining at home. Dipping veggies as well as bread cubes makes fondue a healthier treat. Can't find Gruyère or Emmentaler cheese? Just substitute a high-quality Swiss or Jarlsberg. The flavor will be milder, but just as tasty.

`15 minutes` `30 minutes` `45 minutes`

STEAMED VEGETABLES

8 baby potatoes

8 baby carrots

8 medium-sized asparagus spears, tough ends trimmed and remainder cut in half

8 cauliflower florets

FONDUE

2 tablespoons unbleached all-purpose flour

½ cup low-sodium vegetable stock

8 ounces Gruyère or Emmentaler cheese, grated or cubed (3 cups)

1 clove garlic, cut in half

Pinch nutmeg

Eight 2-inch chunks crusty bread

1 *To make Steamed Vegetables:* Put potatoes on microwave-safe plate, cover with plastic wrap and microwave on high 1 minute. Arrange carrots, asparagus, and cauliflower on plate. Cover veggies with plastic wrap, and heat on high power 4 minutes, or until tender.

2 *To make Fondue:* Measure flour into microwave-safe bowl. Stir in stock gradually to prevent lumps. Add cheese and garlic. Cover, and microwave on high 2 minutes. Stir, then cook 2 to 3 minutes more, or until smooth and no cheese lumps remain. Remove garlic pieces, and stir in nutmeg. Serve immediately with bread chunks and steamed vegetables.

Per Serving: 391 cal; 22g prot; 19g total fat (11g sat. fat); 31g carb; 61mg chol; 350mg sod; 3g fiber; 5g sugars

Cheese-Stuffed Love Apples

SERVES 2

Even in winter, you can find good cherry tomatoes—once known as love apples. They make perfect vessels for the sumptuous herbed goat cheese filling. Toss any leftover cheese mixture with hot pasta, or spread it on sandwiches.

15 minutes **30 minutes** 45 minutes

½ cup nonfat or low-fat cottage cheese

4 ounces soft, fresh goat cheese

2 tablespoons plain nonfat yogurt

¼ to ½ cup chopped fresh herbs (such as parsley, tarragon, dillweed and chives), or to taste

Salt to taste

Freshly ground black pepper to taste

10 cherry tomatoes

10 small fresh dillweed sprigs, for garnish

1 Put cottage cheese and goat cheese in food processor fitted with steel blade, and purée until smooth. Add yogurt, and process 1 to 2 minutes more, or until very smooth. Scrape into small bowl, and stir in herbs, salt and pepper. Set aside.

2 Cut off thin slice from top of each cherry tomato. Using small spoon, scoop out seeds and flesh from centers. Lightly salt insides of tomatoes, and invert on rack set in sink. Drain 5 to 10 minutes.

3 Spoon herbed cheese into each tomato, garnish with dillweed sprig and serve, or refrigerate until serving time.

Per Serving: 220 cal; 19g prot; 12g total fat (8g sat. fat); 9g carb; 30mg chol; 450mg sod; 1g fiber; 6g sugars

Sesame Wonton Wedges

SERVES 6   VEGAN

These are a cinch to make and taste great plain or dipped into hummus or baba ghanoush (eggplant dip). You'll find it hard to believe they contain almost no fat. You can multiply the recipe easily. Wonton wrappers are available in most supermarkets.

15 minutes

¼ cup sesame seeds

½ teaspoon garlic powder

½ teaspoon salt

½ teaspoon ground paprika

30 wonton wrappers, cut in half diagonally

Nonstick cooking spray

1 Preheat oven to 375°F.

2 Mix sesame seeds, garlic powder, salt and paprika in small bowl. Place wonton triangles on baking sheets, and lightly spray them with nonstick cooking spray. Sprinkle spice mixture evenly over triangles.

3 Bake 4 minutes, or until crisp and golden. Transfer to wire rack and let cool completely. Store in airtight container for up to 7 days.

Per Serving: 150 cal; 5g prot; 4g total fat (0.5g sat. fat); 24g carb; 5mg chol; 430mg sod; 2g fiber; 0g sugars

Herbed Goat Cheese and Cucumber Tea Sandwiches

SERVES 8

The cucumber sandwich is the aristocrat of the tea table: cool, gracious and proper. Here, it's given a modern and flavorful twist with herbed goat cheese, and cucumber slices acting as the top piece of "bread."

15 minutes **30 minutes** 45 minutes

8 thin slices whole wheat bread

8 ounces soft goat cheese, at room temperature

3 tablespoons finely chopped fresh parsley

2 tablespoons finely chopped fresh tarragon

2 tablespoons finely chopped fresh chives

1 teaspoon grated lemon zest

½ teaspoon freshly ground black pepper

24 thin slices English cucumber

1 bunch watercress

1 Using 2¼-inch round cookie cutter, cut 24 circles from bread slices (3 rounds per slice).

2 Put goat cheese, parsley, tarragon, chives, lemon zest and pepper in large, resealable plastic bag. Close bag, and squeeze ingredients until well combined.

3 Snip off one corner of bag. Squeeze dollops of goat cheese mixture onto bread circles. Press cucumber slices into cheese, and top with sprigs of watercress. Serve immediately.

Per Serving: 100 cal; 7g prot; 6g total fat (4g sat. fat); 5g carb; 15mg chol; 150mg sod; <1g fiber; 2g sugars

Gruyère, Apricot Jam and Toasted Walnut Panini

SERVES 8

It may seem like an unusual combination, but the salty nuttiness of the Gruyère marries perfectly with the sweet-tart apricot jam. If you can find walnut bread, you can omit the toasted nuts. This recipe requires a panini maker.

¼ cup walnuts

8 slices bread, preferably ½-inch thick, cut from large French round loaf

4 teaspoons apricot jam

6 ounces Gruyère cheese, thinly sliced

1 Preheat panini maker. Preheat oven to 350°F.

2 Put walnuts on baking sheet, and bake for 8 to 10 minutes, or until fragrant. Let cool, and finely chop.

3 Spread 4 slices bread with 1 teaspoon jam each. Sprinkle walnuts on top of jam, and top with one-quarter of Gruyère slices. Cover with remaining bread. Place sandwiches in panini maker, and bake 2 to 4 minutes, or until golden brown and cheese has melted. Slice each sandwich into 4 wedges, and serve warm.

Per Serving: 208 cal; 10g prot; 10g total fat (4g sat. fat); 20g carb; 23mg chol; 294mg sod; 1g fiber; 2g sugars

Smoked Mozzarella Canapés

SERVES 8

The garlic-flavored baguette toasts that form the base for these canapés may be made up to 4 days ahead and kept in a sealable plastic bag at room temperature.

15 minutes **30 minutes** 45 minutes

6 plum tomatoes, seeded and diced

⅓ cup finely chopped kalamata olives

¼ cup finely chopped fresh basil

1 tablespoon minced shallot

3 tablespoons extra-virgin olive oil, divided

1 teaspoon fresh lemon juice

Salt to taste

Freshly ground black pepper to taste

Twenty-four ¼-inch-thick baguette slices

1 to 2 cloves garlic, peeled

8 ounces smoked mozzarella cheese, cut into 24 thin slices

1 Preheat oven to 325°F.

2 Mix tomatoes, olives, basil, shallot, 1 tablespoon olive oil and lemon juice in medium-sized bowl. Season to taste with salt and pepper.

3 Arrange baguette slices in one layer on large baking sheet. Lightly brush slices with remaining 2 tablespoons oil, and season to taste with salt. Toast slices 15 minutes, or until golden, and transfer to rack to cool completely.

4 Lightly rub each bread slice with garlic clove. Arrange a slice of mozzarella on each toast, and top with 1 tablespoon tomato mixture.

Per Serving: 190 cal; 9g prot; 13g total fat (4.5g sat. fat); 9g carb; 15mg chol; 300mg sod; <1g fiber; 1g sugars

Miso-Edamame Bites

SERVES 12   VEGAN

Here's an hors d'oeuvre for all those sushi lovers out there. It's a whole lot easier to put together than an avocado roll, plus the topping can be made up to 24 hours ahead. If you're not into the hot, spicy flavor of wasabi, use plain rice crackers for the toast base.

15 minutes | **30 minutes** | 45 minutes

2½ cups frozen shelled edamame

1 cup thinly sliced green onions (about 2 bunches), divided

2 tablespoons red or yellow miso

2 tablespoons ginger juice from jar of pickled ginger

24 wasabi-flavored rice crackers

24 slices pickled ginger

1 Cook edamame according to package directions, omitting salt. Drain, and reserve ½ cup cooking water.

2 Put 1 cup cooked edamame, ½ cup green onions, miso, ginger juice and reserved cooking water in food processor. Purée until smooth. Transfer to large bowl, and stir in remaining edamame and green onions. Cover with plastic wrap, and chill for up to 24 hours, until ready to assemble.

3 Spoon 2 teaspoons edamame mixture onto each rice cracker. Top with ginger slices, and serve.

Per Serving: 79 cal; 5g prot; 2.5g total fat (0.5g sat. fat); 9g carb; 0mg chol; 240mg sod; 2g fiber; 2g sugars

Perfect Potato Latkes

SERVES 8

Serve these delectable potato cakes with cinnamon-spiked applesauce and vegan sour cream.

15 minutes   30 minutes   **45** minutes

4 cups peeled and quartered baking potatoes (about 4 medium-sized)

1 medium-sized yellow onion, quartered

12.3-ounces light silken tofu

¼ cup nutritional yeast

2½ tablespoons whole wheat flour

2 tablespoons whole-grain yellow cornmeal

1 tablespoon egg replacer powder

1 teaspoon baking powder

1 teaspoon sea salt

½ cup plain soymilk

½ cup dried potato flakes

1 tablespoon olive oil

Nonstick cooking spray

1 Preheat oven to 200°F.

2 Grate potatoes in food processor or using small holes of box grater. Spread on layered paper towels, and press out excess moisture. Grate onion; mix with potatoes in large bowl. Set aside.

3 Put tofu in food processor, and purée until smooth. Add yeast, flour, cornmeal, egg replacer, baking powder and salt. Pour soymilk through feed tube with motor running, and process until blended, 1 to 2 minutes.

4 Add tofu mixture, potato flakes and oil to potato mixture, and mix well. Coat large nonstick skillet with nonstick cooking spray, and heat about 30 seconds over medium heat. Add batter to pan in quarter cupfuls. Cook latkes 3 minutes on each side, or until golden brown. Transfer to baking sheet, cover with foil and keep warm in oven. Repeat, re-spraying pan as necessary. Serve hot.

Per Serving: 140 cal; 6g prot; 2.5g total fat (0g sat. fat); 23g carb; 0mg chol; 380mg sod; 3g fiber; 2g sugars

Corn Blinis with Eggplant and Roasted Pepper Compote

SERVES 8

> These slightly sweet, tender corn blinis will become a staple in your recipe collection. The savory-sweet eggplant compote makes the perfect topping for the blinis.

 45 minutes

COMPOTE

2 tablespoons olive oil

½ cup diced yellow onion

¼ teaspoon crushed red pepper

2 cloves garlic, minced (2 teaspoons)

1 medium-sized Japanese eggplant, cut into ¼-inch dice (about 2 cups)

3 roasted red peppers, drained and finely chopped (about ¾ cup)

1 tablespoon tomato paste

1 teaspoon balsamic vinegar

½ teaspoon sugar

Salt to taste

Freshly ground black pepper to taste

BLINIS

1 cup unbleached all-purpose flour

⅓ cup cornmeal

1 tablespoon sugar

¾ teaspoon baking powder

½ teaspoon salt

¼ teaspoon baking soda

1¼ cups buttermilk

1 large egg

1 tablespoon butter, melted

½ cup corn kernels

Nonstick cooking spray

Per Serving: 198 cal; 6g prot; 6.5g total fat (2g sat. fat); 28g carb; 33mg chol; 588mg sod; 2g fiber; 6g sugars

1 *To make Compote:* Heat oil in large nonstick skillet over medium-high heat. Add onion and crushed red pepper, and sauté 3 to 5 minutes. Stir in garlic, and cook 1 minute more. Add eggplant, reduce heat to medium and cook 5 minutes, stirring often. Add roasted peppers, tomato paste, vinegar, sugar and ⅓ cup water, and cook 5 to 7 minutes more, or until eggplant is tender. Season to taste with salt and pepper, and set aside.

2 *To make Blinis:* Whisk flour, cornmeal, sugar, baking powder, salt, and baking soda together in medium-sized bowl. Whisk buttermilk, egg and melted butter in measuring cup. Stir buttermilk mixture into flour mixture. Fold in corn.

3 Coat large nonstick skillet with nonstick cooking spray, and heat over medium heat. Scoop batter onto skillet using ¼-cup measuring cup. Cook for 2 minutes on each side, or until blinis are golden brown. Repeat with remaining batter, respraying pan as necessary.

4 Top blinis with compote. Serve warm.

4

Salads

Grilled Asparagus Vinaigrette

SERVES 6

VEGAN

For grilling, we prefer asparagus with thick stems, but the pencil-thin spears are perfectly acceptable.

VINAIGRETTE

2 tablespoons red or white wine vinegar

1 tablespoon chopped fresh basil

2 cloves garlic, minced (2 teaspoons)

½ teaspoon Dijon mustard

½ teaspoon salt

¼ teaspoon freshly ground black pepper

¼ cup extra virgin olive oil

SALAD

1 small head Boston or butter lettuce, rinsed, dried and separated into individual leaves

1 to 1¼ pounds asparagus, ends trimmed

Shaved Parmesan cheese, for garnish, optional

1 Prepare medium-hot charcoal fire, or preheat gas grill (or broiler).

2 *To make Vinaigrette:* Combine vinegar, basil, garlic, mustard, salt and pepper in small bowl. Slowly pour in olive oil, whisking until oil is fully incorporated. Set aside.

3 *To make Salad:* Divide lettuce among 6 plates, or arrange on large platter.

4 Brush asparagus with vinaigrette. Grill, turning occasionally, until asparagus is tender and grill-marked, about 8 minutes.

5 Arrange asparagus on lettuce. Drizzle with remaining vinaigrette. Garnish with Parmesan, if using, and serve.

Per Serving: 100 cal; 1g prot; 9g total fat (1.5g sat. fat); 3g carb; 0mg chol; 210mg sod; <1g fiber; 1g sugars

Creamy Lime-Cheddar Dressing

MAKES ABOUT ⅔ CUP

This delicious dressing is especially good with our Chipotle Portobello Salad (page 72).

15 minutes · 30 minutes · 45 minutes

¼ cup plain soymilk

¼ cup extra virgin olive oil

¼ cup grated aged white cheddar cheese or soy cheddar cheese

2 tablespoons fresh lime juice

1 tablespoon white miso or 1 teaspoon vegetarian Worcestershire sauce

2 green onions (white and most of green parts), chopped

1 medium-sized clove garlic

Freshly ground black pepper to taste

1 In food processor or blender, combine soymilk, olive oil, cheese, lime juice, miso, green onions and garlic, and process until smooth and creamy.

2 Transfer to small bowl, and season to taste with black pepper. Use immediately, or store in an airtight container in the refrigerator for up to 7 days.

Per Tablespoon: 56 cal; 1g prot; 5g total fat (0.5g sat. fat); 1g carb; <1mg chol; 73mg sod; <1g fiber; <1g sugars

Extra-Healthy Spinach Salad

SERVES 8

This irresistible salad is crammed with hard-to-get vegetarian goodies: protein, calcium, iron—even vitamin B12. You will have extra dressing, which you can pass on the side or store in the refrigerator for up to 7 days.

15 minutes | **30 minutes** | 45 minutes

TOFU CROUTONS

4 ounces extra-firm herb tofu

1 large egg

¼ cup unbleached all-purpose flour

3 teaspoons garlic salt

1 teaspoon onion powder

½ teaspoon freshly ground black pepper

3 tablespoons canola oil

SALAD DRESSING

½ cup canola oil

½ cup white wine vinegar

½ cup granulated sugar

3 tablespoons mandarin orange juice

SPINACH SALAD

1½ cups fresh baby spinach, rinsed and dried

1½ cups mesclun salad mix, rinsed and dried

One 15-ounce can mandarin oranges, drained and juice reserved

One 7-ounce can chickpeas, drained and rinsed

1 cup crumbled feta cheese

½ cup walnuts

½ cup dried cranberries

1 red bell pepper, cut in ¼-inch slices

Per Serving: 330 cal; 9g prot; 21g total fat (4.5g sat. fat); 26g carb; 44mg chol; 746mg sod; 4g fiber; 12g sugars

1 *To make Tofu Croutons:* Preheat oven to 350°F. Bake tofu 20 minutes. When dry, cut into crouton-size cubes.

2 Beat egg in small bowl. Combine flour, garlic salt, onion powder and black pepper in medium-sized bowl. Dip tofu cubes in egg, and dust with flour mixture.

3 Heat oil in pan over medium-high heat. Sauté tofu cubes about 10 minutes, until golden and crispy on all sides. Cool.

4 *To make Salad Dressing:* Combine all the ingredients in small nonreactive pot. Cook over medium heat 2 to 3 minutes, until sugar dissolves. Transfer to cruet. Let cool.

5 *To make Spinach Salad:* Put all the salad ingredients in large bowl. Add half of dressing, toss well and garnish with croutons. Serve immediately.

Spinach and Blue Cheese Salad

SERVES 6

Artisanal cheese makers across America are winning international awards for their blue cheeses, so we thought we'd honor them with a tangy salad of apples and sunflower seeds.

15 minutes **30 minutes** 45 minutes

CIDER VINAIGRETTE

2 tablespoons cider vinegar

1 tablespoon Dijon mustard

1 tablespoon honey

½ teaspoon salt

¼ teaspoon freshly ground black pepper

3 tablespoons olive oil

1 shallot, minced (about 3 tablespoons)

SALAD

¼ cup shelled sunflower seeds

16-oz. bag baby spinach, rinsed and dried

1 large apple, thinly sliced

½ cup crumbled blue cheese

1 *To make Cider Vinaigrette:* Combine vinegar, mustard, honey, salt and pepper in small bowl. Whisk in oil and 2 tablespoons water. Stir in shallots.

2 *To make Salad:* Put sunflower seeds in medium-sized skillet. Toast over medium heat 5 to 6 minutes, or until browned and fragrant, shaking pan often. Transfer to small bowl, and cool.

3 Just before serving, toss spinach, apple, cheese and sunflower seeds with vinaigrette. Divide salad among 6 plates, and serve.

Per Serving: 149 cal; 4g prot; 11.5g total fat
(2g sat. fat); 10g carb; 4mg chol; 309mg sod; 4g fiber;
7g sugars

Mixed Greens with Hazelnut Oil Vinaigrette

SERVES 6   VEGAN

This luxurious dressing polishes the salad leaves with a shiny coat. If you can't find blanched (skinless) hazelnuts, see the note on how to prepare them.

15 minutes **30** minutes **45** minutes

1 cup blanched hazelnuts, coarsely chopped

2 tablespoons maple syrup

2 tablespoons unrefined sugar, such as maple sugar, Sucanat or evaporated cane juice

⅓ cup balsamic vinegar

½ teaspoon Dijon mustard

¼ cup toasted hazelnut oil

8 cups mesclun salad mix, rinsed and dried

Salt to taste

Freshly ground black pepper to taste

Note: To remove skins from hazelnuts, put nuts on baking sheet, and bake at 350°F 8 to 10 minutes, until skins start to loosen. Wrap hazelnuts in kitchen towel, and rub against each other to loosen skins. Transfer cleaned hazelnuts to bowl.

1 Preheat oven to 350°F. Line a baking sheet with parchment paper.

2 Combine hazelnuts, maple syrup and sugar in medium-sized bowl. Spread nuts on baking sheet, and bake 15 minutes, stirring once, until caramelized. Let cool.

3 Pour vinegar into small saucepan. Bring to a boil, reduce heat and simmer 5 to 7 minutes, uncovered, or until liquid is reduced to 2 tablespoons.

4 Pour vinegar into small bowl, and stir in mustard. Slowly drizzle hazelnut oil into bowl, whisking constantly until well blended. Let cool.

5 Put greens in large bowl, and sprinkle with salt and pepper to taste. Toss with dressing. Sprinkle with caramelized hazelnuts, and serve.

Per Serving: 280 cal; 4g prot; 23g total fat (1.5g sat. fat); 19g carb; 0mg chol; 35mg sod; 4g fiber; 13g sugars

Strawberry Salad with Gorgonzola Dressing

SERVES 6

Gorgonzola dolce is a creamy blue cheese from the north of Italy that is milder and less salty than French Roquefort. It makes a tart, creamy dressing for this salad of tender lettuce and sliced spring berries. The slight bitterness of watercress adds a note of contrast, and the optional toasted almonds provide both crunch and sweetness.

15 minutes **30 minutes** 45 minutes

DRESSING

¼ cup Gorgonzola dolce cheese, at room temperature

½ cup low-fat plain yogurt

2 tablespoons fresh lemon juice

1 tablespoon vegetable oil

Salt to taste

Freshly ground black pepper to taste

SALAD

1 large head butter lettuce, or 2 heads Bibb lettuce, rinsed, dried and leaves separated

1 bunch watercress, washed, dried and stemmed, optional

18 fresh large mint leaves, cut into thin strips

2 cups or 1 pint basket strawberries, washed, hulled and sliced

Salt to taste

¼ cup slivered almonds, toasted, optional

1 *To make Dressing:* Put cheese into food processor, and process until soft and smooth. Transfer to small bowl, and whisk in yogurt, lemon juice and oil. If too thick, whisk in 1 tablespoon water. Season to taste with salt and pepper. Set aside.

2 *To make Salad:* Tear lettuce into bite-sized pieces. Put lettuce, watercress, if using, mint and berries into large bowl, and season with salt. Add dressing, toss well and arrange on salad plates. Garnish with toasted almonds, if using, and serve.

Per Serving: 90 cal; 4g prot; 6g total fat (2g sat. fat); 7g carb; 10mg chol; 115mg sod; 1g fiber; 4g sugars

Frisée and Endive Salad with Olive Vinaigrette

SERVES 6 VEGAN

Kalamata olives plus red wine vinegar, garlic and fresh parsley add up to a bold dressing that complements the assertive greens.

SALAD

6 tablespoons sliced almonds

4 cups frisée leaves, rinsed, dried and trimmed

2 heads (8 ounces) Belgian endive, rinsed, dried and leaves thinly sliced

2 stalks celery, cut into thin 3-inch-long strips

VINAIGRETTE

3 tablespoons olive oil

1 tablespoon red wine vinegar

½ tablespoon fresh lemon juice

1 clove garlic

Freshly ground black pepper to taste

½ cup pitted kalamata olives, coarsely chopped

⅛ cup chopped fresh parsley

1 *To make Salad:* Toast almonds in small heavy-bottomed skillet over medium heat, stirring often, 5 to 7 minutes, or until golden. Set aside.

2 Combine frisée, endive and celery in large bowl; toss to mix.

3 *To make Vinaigrette:* Put olive oil, vinegar, lemon juice, garlic and pepper to taste in blender or food processor, and blend until smooth. Add olives and parsley, and pulse to combine.

4 Add dressing to greens, and toss well. Divide salad among serving plates, and sprinkle each with 1 tablespoon almonds. Serve immediately.

Per Serving: 140 cal; 2g prot; 12.5g total fat (1.5g sat. fat); 6g carb; 0mg chol; 189mg sod; 3g fiber; 1g sugars

Endive, Pear and Walnut Salad with Raspberry Vinaigrette

SERVES 6

This salad calls for Asian pears, also known as Chinese or apple pears. They combine the sweet, mellow flavor of a pear with the crispness of an apple. They're available at many large supermarkets, but if you can't find them, Bartlett or Anjou pears are equally delicious.

15 minutes 30 minutes 45 minutes

RASPBERRY VINAIGRETTE

2 tablespoons raspberry vinegar

1 tablespoon honey

1 teaspoon Dijon mustard

1½ tablespoons extra virgin olive oil

2 teaspoons flaxseed oil

¼ teaspoon fine sea salt

⅛ teaspoon freshly ground white pepper

ENDIVE, PEAR AND WALNUT SALAD

4 medium-sized heads (16 ounces) red Belgian endive, rinsed, dried and leaves cut into 1-inch pieces

1 bunch watercress, rinsed, dried and torn into small pieces

1 large Asian pear, peeled, cored and thinly sliced

½ cup chopped walnuts, toasted

1 *To make Raspberry Vinaigrette:* Whisk together vinegar, honey and mustard in small bowl. Slowly whisk in 1 tablespoon water and oils until emulsified. Season with salt and pepper. Set aside.

2 *To make Endive, Pear & Walnut Salad:* Toss endive and watercress in large bowl. Re-whisk vinaigrette just before serving; pour over salad greens, tossing to coat. Divide salad among 6 serving plates. Top each with pear slices and walnuts, and serve.

Per Serving: 150 cal; 2g prot; 11g total fat (1g sat. fat); 12g carb; 0mg chol; 125mg sod; 3g fiber; 7g sugars

Winter Salad with Beets, Avocado and Orange with Citrus Vinaigrette

SERVES 4 VEGAN

The orange vinaigrette alone is reason enough to make this salad. Prepared beets are available in the produce section of many grocery stores, but you can often also find them at the salad bar.

15 minutes 30 minutes 45 minutes

VINAIGRETTE

½ cup orange juice

3 teaspoons champagne vinegar

1 finely chopped shallot (2 teaspoons)

2 tablespoons olive oil

Salt to taste

Freshly ground black pepper to taste

WINTER SALAD

8 ounces cooked beets, cut into small wedges (about 2 cups)

Salt to taste

Freshly ground black pepper to taste

1 cup orange sections

3 cups mixed baby greens, rinsed and dried

1 ripe Hass avocado, sliced into thin wedges

1 *To make Vinaigrette:* Place small saucepan over medium heat, and add orange juice and 1 teaspoon vinegar. Bring to a simmer, and cook 7 to 9 minutes, or until it has thickened and reduced down to 3 tablespoons Pour orange reduction over chopped shallot in small bowl. Whisk in remaining vinegar and olive oil. Season to taste with salt and pepper.

2 *To make Winter Salad:* Toss beets with 1 tablespoon of vinaigrette, and season with salt and pepper. Add orange sections and greens, and toss with ¼ cup vinaigrette. Scatter avocado wedges on top of salad. Serve immediately.

Per Serving: 201 cal; 3g prot; 13.5g total fat (2g sat. fat); 20g carb; 0mg chol; 199mg sod; 6g fiber; 12g sugars

Clementine-Fennel Salad with Clementine Vinaigrette

SERVES 6   VEGAN

For this midwinter salad, be sure to include a variety of greens, including some that are slightly bitter, such as arugula—they contrast wonderfully with the sweet clementines.

15 minutes | 30 minutes | 45 minutes

DRESSING

3 clementines

2 tablespoons white wine vinegar

2 tablespoons fresh lemon juice, or more to taste

½ teaspoon salt

¼ teaspoon freshly ground black pepper

3 tablespoons olive oil

1 tablespoon vegetable, canola or safflower oil

SALAD

6 to 8 cups loosely packed mixed greens, rinsed and dried

2 large fennel bulbs, trimmed and chopped (reserve fronds for garnish)

3 Belgian endive, rinsed, dried and chopped

4 clementines, peeled and sectioned

Fennel fronds for garnish, optional

¼ cup toasted pine nuts, optional

1 *To make Dressing:* Grate zest from 1 clementine, and set aside. Cut all clementines in half, and squeeze out about ½ cup juice total.

2 Combine clementine juice, vinegar, lemon juice, salt and pepper in large bowl, and whisk until salt dissolves. Add oils in slow, steady stream, whisking well. Taste for seasoning, adding more lemon juice if too sweet.

3 *To make Salad:* Add greens, fennel, endive and clementines to bowl with dressing, and toss gently to mix. Arrange on salad plates, garnish with fennel fronds, and sprinkle with pine nuts, if using. Serve immediately.

Per Serving: 180 cal; 3g prot; 10g total fat (1g sat. fat); 27g carb; 0mg chol; 250mg sod; 8g fiber; 15g sugars

Romaine Salad with Avocado "Caesar" Dressing

SERVES 6   VEGAN

This salad is wonderful as is, but for a delicious variation, try adding roasted corn and roasted red peppers.

15 minutes **30 minutes** 45 minutes

AVOCADO "CAESAR" DRESSING

1 teaspoon whole cumin seeds

1 ripe medium-sized Hass avocado, peeled and pitted

3 tablespoons fresh lime juice

3 tablespoons extra-virgin olive oil

1 clove garlic, minced (1 teaspoon)

½ teaspoon salt

¼ teaspoon Dijon mustard

Freshly ground black pepper to taste

Pinch cayenne pepper

SALAD

1 tablespoon olive oil

Two 6-inch corn tortillas, cut into strips

Salt to taste

12 cups romaine lettuce, rinsed, dried and torn into bite-sized pieces

1 medium-sized tomato, seeded and diced

1 *To make Avocado "Caesar" Dressing:* In small skillet, toast cumin seeds, stirring often, until fragrant, about 2 minutes. Using spice grinder or mortar and pestle, pulverize.

2 Put cumin, avocado, lime juice, oil, garlic, salt, mustard and ¼ cup water into food processor, and purée until smooth; add more water, if needed. Season with pepper and cayenne.

3 *To make Salad:* Line plate with paper towel. Heat oil in medium-sized nonstick skillet over medium heat. Add tortilla strips, and cook, stirring constantly, until crisp and lightly golden, about 2 minutes. Transfer strips to paper towels, and drain. Sprinkle with salt.

4 Toss lettuce with tomato and dressing in large bowl. Transfer mixture to individual plates, top with tortilla strips, and serve.

Per Serving: 190 cal; 3g prot; 15g total fat (2g sat. fat); 12g carb; 0mg chol; 230mg sod; 5g fiber; 2g sugars

Waldorf Salad

For this salad, you can either peel the apples and pears, or not.

15 minutes 30 minutes **45 minutes**

⅔ cup apple cider

⅔ cup plain low-fat yogurt

¼ teaspoon ground cinnamon

2 cups chopped apples, such as
   Granny Smith, Rome and/or Gala

2 cups chopped pears, such as Bosc

1 cup seedless grapes, halved

½ cup chopped celery

½ cup golden raisins

⅓ cup coarsely chopped pecans,
   toasted

6 Boston lettuce leaves, rinsed and
   dried

1 Bring cider to a boil over high heat in small saucepan. Cook until reduced to about 3 table-spoons, 15 to 20 minutes. Cool completely.

2 Mix yogurt and cinnamon into cider until blended. Set aside.

3 Mix apples, pears, grapes, celery, raisins and pecans in large bowl. Add yogurt mixture, tossing to coat. Line plates with lettuce leaves, top with salad, and serve.

Per Serving: 180 cal; 3g prot; 6g total fat (0.5g sat. fat); 33g carb; 0mg chol; 35mg sod; 4g fiber; 26g sugars

Tofu Niçoise Salad

SERVES 4   VEGAN

Mushrooms and green beans replace the customary potatoes in this salad, adding complex carbs and extra fiber. The fresh citrus juice brightens a prepared dressing.

15 minutes   30 minutes   45 minutes

¼ cup low-fat Italian dressing, such as Newman's Own

1 tablespoon fresh lemon juice

1 clove garlic, minced (1 teaspoon)

⅛ teaspoon freshly ground black pepper

6 cups baby salad greens, rinsed and dried

4 medium-sized tomatoes, each cut into 4 wedges

1 pound Italian-style baked tofu, cut into 16 slices

4 ounces baby green beans, steamed and chilled

4 medium-sized white button mushrooms, thinly sliced

16 niçoise olives

1 Whisk together Italian dressing, lemon juice, garlic and pepper. Let stand 10 minutes.

2 Divide salad greens among 4 large salad plates. Arrange 4 tomato wedges and 4 slices of tofu on top of each. Divide green beans equally among salads. Scatter mushrooms and 4 olives on each salad. Drizzle each with 1 tablespoon dressing, and serve.

Per Serving: 260 cal; 21g prot; 14g total fat (2.5g sat. fat); 17g carb; 0mg chol; 830mg sod; 8g fiber; 6g sugars

Asian Chopped Salad

SERVES 6   VEGAN

Chopped salads are so easy to assemble and eat that they should become part of every cook's repertoire. This nutritious version puts an Asian spin on the theme. Offer crisp breadsticks and iced green tea as accompaniments.

15 minutes 30 minutes 45 minutes

8 ounces Asian-style baked tofu, diced

1 red bell pepper, diced

1 cup cooked shelled edamame

½ cup wasabi peas

½ cup soy nuts

1 cucumber, peeled and diced

1 tablespoon minced peeled fresh ginger, or more to taste

1 tablespoon toasted sesame seeds

Tamari Asian-style salad dressing to taste

1 In large bowl, combine tofu, red pepper, edamame, peas and soy nuts.

2 Squeeze diced cucumber to remove excess moisture, and add to bowl. Sprinkle salad with ginger and sesame seeds. Toss with desired amount of dressing, and serve.

Per Serving: 180 cal; 16g prot; 8g total fat (1g sat. fat); 13g carb; 0mg chol; 200mg sod; 4g fiber; 3g sugars

Watercress, Orange and Olive Salad

This refreshing salad makes a lively accompaniment for just about any Mediterranean dish, including pizza.

15 minutes **30** minutes **45** minutes

VINAIGRETTE

⅛ cup fresh orange juice

⅛ cup red wine vinegar

2 shallots, finely chopped

Salt to taste

Freshly ground black pepper to taste

Pinch granulated sugar

½ cup olive oil

SALAD

2 bunches watercress or arugula, rinsed, dried and stems trimmed

3 navel oranges

18 whole kalamata olives

3 tablespoons toasted pine nuts

1 *To make Vinaigrette:* Whisk together orange juice and vinegar in small bowl. Stir in shallots, salt, pepper and sugar. Let stand 15 minutes. Whisk in oil; set aside.

2 *To make Salad:* Toss watercress in large bowl with about ½ cup vinaigrette, and arrange on 6 plates. Peel oranges, and remove all pith. Cut between segments, removing membranes and seeds. Toss segments in bowl with 1 tablespoon vinaigrette, and arrange on top of watercress. Scatter with olives and pine nuts. Drizzle with remaining vinaigrette, and serve.

Per Serving: 270 cal; 2g prot; 24g total fat (3g sat. fat); 13g carb; 0mg chol; 200mg sod; 2g fiber; 7g sugars

Persian Cucumber and Tomato Salad

Known as *shirazi* salad, this refreshing combination calls for Persian cucumbers, which are small, crunchy and sweet. You may substitute small pickling cucumbers; just peel them first. For even more flavor, add a few tablespoons of chopped mint and green onions to the salad and some extra squeezes of lemon juice to the dressing.

15 minutes 30 minutes 45 minutes

DRESSING

2 tablespoons olive oil

2 tablespoons fresh lemon juice

¼ teaspoon sea salt

¼ teaspoon freshly ground black pepper

SALAD

5 small cucumbers, preferably Persian, unpeeled and diced, or 5 small cucumbers, peeled and diced

¼ yellow onion, diced

1 large tomato, diced

¼ cup fresh parsley, finely chopped

1 *To make Dressing:* Whisk together all the ingredients in small bowl.

2 *To make Salad:* Combine all the ingredients in large bowl. Toss with dressing, and serve.

Per Serving: 50 cal; 1g prot; 3.5g total fat (0g sat. fat); 4g carb; 0mg chol; 75mg sod; 1g fiber; 2g sugars

Spinach-Shiitake Salad

SERVES 4 TO 6   VEGAN

The shiitakes shrivel and crisp as they roast and taste almost smoky.

15 minutes | 30 minutes | **45** minutes

SPINACH-SHIITAKE SALAD

8 ounces fresh shiitake mushrooms, stems removed and caps cut into ½-inch-thick slices

2 tablespoons extra virgin olive oil

2 tablespoons tamari or low-sodium soy sauce

1 medium-sized navel orange

4½ cups fresh baby spinach leaves, rinsed and dried

LEMON-ROSEMARY VINAIGRETTE

1 medium-sized clove garlic, minced and mashed to a paste with ¼ teaspoon salt

1 tablespoon fresh lemon juice

1 tablespoon balsamic vinegar

1 teaspoon minced fresh rosemary

1 teaspoon grated lemon zest

½ teaspoon Dijon mustard

1 tablespoon tamari or low-sodium soy sauce

4 tablespoons olive oil

Freshly ground black pepper to taste

1 Preheat oven to 375°F. Line baking sheet with parchment paper or aluminum foil.

2 *To make Spinach-Shiitake Salad:* Toss mushrooms with oil and tamari. Put mushrooms on baking sheet, and bake, tossing once, 30 minutes, or until brown and crispy. Set aside.

3 Cut disk off top and bottom of orange, and remove all peel and pith. Cut orange crosswise into 5 rings. Cut up rings by cutting between sections. Put mushrooms, orange pieces and spinach in large bowl.

4 *To make Lemon-Rosemary Vinaigrette:* Put garlic paste, lemon juice, vinegar, rosemary, lemon zest, mustard and tamari in small bowl. Thoroughly whisk in oil. Add pepper to taste.

5 Pour vinaigrette over salad, and toss. Serve immediately.

Per Serving: 170 cal; 3g prot; 14g total fat (2g sat. fat); 8g carb; 0mg chol; 650mg sod; 2g fiber; 3g sugars

Corn Salad

SERVES 6 VEGAN

Based on sweet, fresh corn, this salad says "summer." If the corn is very moist and sweet, use it raw. If not, blanch the kernels in boiling water for 1 minute. Drain, and refresh them in cold water to stop the cooking. The salad will hold up for hours and tastes best at room temperature.

15 minutes 30 minutes 45 minutes

6 tablespoons olive oil, divided

1 cup finely minced red onion

2 teaspoons chili powder

1 teaspoon ground cumin

3 cups fresh corn kernels (6 ears)

1 red bell pepper, diced

1 green bell pepper, diced

1 to 1½ cups peeled, seeded and diced tomatoes

¼ cup chopped fresh cilantro

3 tablespoons sherry vinegar, or to taste

Salt to taste

Freshly ground black pepper to taste

1 Heat 2 tablespoons oil in medium-sized skillet over medium heat, and cook onion 2 to 3 minutes. Add chili powder and cumin, and cook 1 minute more. Transfer to large bowl to cool. Add corn, peppers and tomatoes to onion. Fold in cilantro.

2 Whisk together remaining 4 tablespoons oil and vinegar in small bowl. Drizzle over salad, and toss to combine well. Season to taste with salt and pepper, and serve.

Per Serving: 300 cal; 4g prot; 27g total fat (3g sat. fat); 22g carb; 0mg chol; 25mg sod; 4g fiber; 6g sugars

Chipotle Portobello Salad

SERVES 8

We like to buy the prepackaged organic romaine hearts for this salad and the long, crostini-shaped packaged croutons that come in clear cellophane bags.

15 minutes **30 minutes** 45 minutes

3 tablespoons olive oil, divided

3 tablespoons fresh lime juice

1 tablespoon tamari or low-sodium soy sauce

½ teaspoon ground chipotle chile

4 large portobello mushrooms, stems removed

Salt to taste

Freshly ground black pepper to taste

Nonstick cooking spray

3 romaine hearts (12 ounces), rinsed, dried and torn into bite-sized pieces

Creamy Lime-Cheddar Dressing (page 55)

One 11-ounce package croutons

1 Whisk together 2 tablespoons olive oil, lime juice, tamari and chipotle chile in large bowl. Season mushrooms with salt and pepper, and brush with chipotle mixture. Let stand 10 minutes.

2 Coat large skillet with nonstick cooking spray, add remaining 1 tablespoon oil and heat over medium-high heat. Add mushrooms, and cook 3 to 4 minutes on each side, or until lightly browned and tender. Transfer mushrooms to cutting board, let cool slightly and cut diagonally into thin slices.

3 Toss romaine with Creamy Lime-Cheddar Dressing in large bowl. Transfer lettuce to serving platter, and top with mushrooms and croutons. Serve immediately.

Per Serving with Dressing: 520 cal; 16g prot; 32g total fat (5g sat. fat); 42g carb; 15mg chol; 1,100mg sod; 3g fiber; 6g sugars

Quinoa Tabbouleh

SERVES 4

VEGAN

You may discover that you like this nutritious, wheat-free variation of this traditional Middle Eastern grain salad even better than the original. Serve it as part of a *meze* (a Mediterranean appetizer) platter with hummus, baba ghanoush (roasted eggplant dip) and pita bread, or mound it on a bed of lettuce with sliced tomatoes on the side.

15 minutes **30 minutes** 45 minutes

1 cup uncooked quinoa, rinsed

½ cup finely chopped fresh parsley

¼ cup fresh lemon juice

2 tablespoons extra virgin olive oil

1 to 2 cloves garlic, minced
(1 to 2 teaspoons)

Salt to taste

1 Combine quinoa and 2 cups water in medium-sized saucepan. Cover, and bring to a boil. Reduce heat, and simmer 15 to 20 minutes, or until quinoa is tender and liquid is absorbed.

2 Put cooked quinoa in large bowl, fluff with fork and let cool. Add all the remaining ingredients, and mix well. Serve tabbouleh chilled or at room temperature.

Per Serving: 231 cal; 6g prot; 9.5g total fat (1g sat. fat); 32g carb; 0mg chol; 304mg sod; 3g fiber; <1g sugars

Fruited Bulgur and Lentil Salad

SERVES 6

VEGAN

This light version of the classic Middle Eastern bulgur salad, or tabbouleh, has a delicious and healthful twist: the addition of dried fruits and red lentils. It's good warm or cold. The recipe makes enough for a great light dinner one night plus lunch-to-go the next day. Add wheat crackers and some shredded lettuce or cabbage, if you like.

15 minutes | 30 minutes | **45 minutes**

1 cup medium uncooked bulgur, rinsed

½ cup (8 ounces) red lentils, picked over and rinsed

½ cup shredded carrots

½ cup chopped dried plums or dates

½ cup chopped dried apricots

⅓ cup chopped fresh parsley

¼ cup chopped fresh mint

3 tablespoons fresh lemon juice

1½ tablespoons olive oil

3 tablespoons toasted pine nuts

Salt to taste

Freshly ground black pepper to taste

1 Bring 1½ cups lightly salted water to a boil in large saucepan. Stir in bulgur. Remove pan from heat, cover and let stand 30 minutes, or until liquid is absorbed. Fluff bulgur with fork, transfer to large bowl and let cool.

2 Meanwhile, combine lentils in small saucepan with enough water to cover by ½ inch. Heat over medium heat, and cook until lentils are tender, about 5 minutes. Drain, rinse under cold running water and drain well.

3 Add lentils, carrots, dried plums, apricots, parsley, mint, lemon juice, oil and pine nuts to bulgur, and toss to mix. Let sit 20 minutes to let flavors meld. Season to taste with salt and pepper, and serve.

Per Serving: 260 cal; 8g prot; 7g total fat (0.5g sat. fat); 45g carb; 0mg chol; 20mg sod; 9g fiber; 13g sugars

Barley with Black Beans

SERVES 6   VEGAN

Almost everyone's familiar with pearl barley, but if you've got 10 extra minutes, consider pot barley too. It's similar in taste to the pearl but larger grained. A bottled balsamic vinaigrette and roasted red peppers give spark to this dish, which you may serve warm or at room temperature. It's superb served with oven-roasted root vegetables and some cornbread.

15 minutes | 30 minutes | **45 minutes**

1 cup uncooked pearl or pot barley, rinsed

One 15.5-ounce can black beans, drained and rinsed

One 12-ounce jar roasted red peppers, drained and sliced

½ cup prepared balsamic vinaigrette

2 tablespoons chopped fresh dillweed, or more to taste

Salt to taste

Freshly ground black pepper to taste

1 Put 3 cups water into large saucepan, and bring to a boil over medium heat. Stir in barley. Cover, reduce heat to low and cook 30 minutes for pearl barley (40 minutes for pot barley), or until water is absorbed. (If grain is too chewy, add another ½ cup water, and cook until water is absorbed.)

2 Combine barley, black beans, roasted red peppers, vinaigrette and dillweed in large bowl. Season to taste with salt and pepper, mix well, and serve.

Per Serving: 300 cal; 8g prot; 10g total fat (1.5g sat. fat); 45g carb; 0mg chol; 580mg sod; 9g fiber; 6g sugars

Red Cabbage Slaw with Baked Tofu and Peanut Dressing

SERVES 6   VEGAN

This recipe showcases the power and versatility of the mini-chopper attachment that comes with today's immersion blenders. It's so strong that it turns unpeeled ginger into a soft pulp, making the ginger-infused peanut dressing for this salad a snap.

15 minutes   30 minutes   45 minutes

PEANUT DRESSING

1 small clove garlic

One 2-inch piece fresh ginger, cut into 8 pieces (peeling unnecessary)

⅓ cup unsalted, nonhydrogenated peanut butter

1½ tablespoons low-sodium tamari

2 teaspoons packed light brown sugar

1 teaspoon apple cider vinegar

RED CABBAGE SLAW

8 ounces Asian-style baked tofu, cut into ½-inch dice

6 cups (12 ounces) shredded red cabbage

1 medium-sized carrot, peeled and grated

½ cup thinly sliced green onions

Salt to taste

Freshly ground black pepper to taste

1 *To make Peanut Dressing:* Put garlic and ginger in mini-chopper beaker, and pulse until finely chopped. Add peanut butter, tamari, brown sugar, vinegar and ¼ cup water, and blend until smooth. Thin with 1 tablespoon water or more, if necessary, so that dressing is pourable.

2 *To make Red Cabbage Slaw:* Combine all the ingredients in a large bowl. Pour dressing over salad, and toss to coat. Season to taste with salt and pepper, and serve.

Per Serving: 186 cal; 11g prot; 10.5g total fat (1.5g sat. fat); 13g carb; 0mg chol; 452mg sod; 4g fiber; 7g sugars

Warm Mushroom Salad with Arugula, Pecorino and Toasted Walnuts

SERVES 4

The warm sautéed mushrooms slightly wilt the arugula in this winter salad. If you can't find or don't like arugula, you may always substitute spinach.

15 minutes **30 minutes** 45 minutes

3 tablespoons olive oil, divided

1 pound cremini or white button mushrooms, quartered

1 small shallot, minced (1 tablespoon)

1 clove garlic, minced (1 teaspoon)

2 tablespoons sherry

Salt to taste

Freshly ground black pepper to taste

1½ tablespoons balsamic vinegar

½ tablespoon sherry vinegar

5 ounces (2½ cups) arugula, rinsed and dried

¼ cup chopped walnuts, toasted

2 ounces pecorino cheese, thinly shaved with vegetable peeler

1 Heat 2 tablespoons oil in large skillet over medium-high heat. Add mushrooms, and cook, stirring occasionally, 10 to 12 minutes, or until mushroom liquid is gone and mushrooms start to caramelize.

2 Add shallot and garlic, and sauté 1 minute. Add sherry, and cook 1 minute more, or until liquid is gone. Season to taste with salt and pepper.

3 Combine vinegars and remaining 1 tablespoon olive oil in small bowl. Pour over mushrooms in pan, and sauté 5 seconds; remove from heat.

4 Put arugula and walnuts in large bowl. Pour mushrooms over greens, and toss to combine. Sprinkle cheese over top, and serve immediately.

Per Serving: 235 cal; 10g prot; 19g total fat (4g sat. fat); 10g carb; 13mg chol; 331mg sod; 2g fiber; 5g sugars

Baked Tomato and Mozzarella Stacks with Arugula, Corn and Balsamic Syrup

SERVES 4 AS SALAD OR 8 AS APPETIZER

This is a different take on the usual mozzarella and tomato salad. Our recipe has warm tomato and mozzarella stacks topped with crunchy breadcrumbs. The balsamic syrup can be made several days ahead.

15 minutes | **30 minutes** | 45 minutes

Nonstick cooking spray

¾ cup balsamic vinegar

4 medium-sized tomatoes, cored

8 ounces fresh mozzarella cheese, cut into 8 slices

4 teaspoons prepared basil pesto

1 slice whole wheat bread

1 tablespoon olive oil

Salt to taste

Freshly ground black pepper to taste

1 cup fresh corn kernels (from 2 ears)

2 cups (4 ounces) arugula, rinsed and dried

1 Preheat oven to 450°F. Spray baking sheet with nonstick cooking spray.

2 Heat vinegar in small saucepan over medium heat. Bring to a simmer, and cook 10 minutes, or until syrup-like and reduced to ⅓ cup. Remove from heat, and set aside.

3 Slice each tomato horizontally into 4 slices. Lay 8 tomato slices on baking sheet. Place 1 slice cheese on each slice tomato. Spread ½ teaspoon pesto on each cheese slice, and top with the remaining tomato slices.

4 Put bread in bowl of food processor, and pulse until fine crumbs. Pour into small bowl, and toss with olive oil and salt and pepper to taste. Sprinkle crumbs on top of tomatoes, and bake 5 to 7 minutes, or until crumbs are golden and cheese is soft.

5 Toss corn and arugula together in medium-sized bowl, and turn out onto serving platter. Place tomato stacks on top, and pass balsamic syrup for each guest to drizzle on top of tomatoes.

Per Serving (Serves 4): 391 cal; 17g prot; 21g total fat (10g sat. fat); 37g carb; 42mg chol; 580mg sod; 3g fiber; 20g sugars

Per Serving (Serves 8): 196 cal; 8g prot; 10.5g total fat (5g sat. fat); 19g carb; 21mg chol; 290mg sod; 2g fiber; 10g sugars

Middle Eastern Couscous Salad with Feta and Mint

SERVES 6

The only "cooking" you do here is boiling water, and you do that in the microwave! If tomato couscous is unavailable, substitute whole wheat, spinach or plain couscous—all are equally delicious.

15 minutes | **30 minutes** | 45 minutes

1⅓ cups uncooked tomato couscous

4 tablespoons extra virgin olive oil

2 red or green jalapeño chiles, seeded and minced

1 teaspoon ground cumin

1 teaspoon ground coriander

2 cloves garlic, minced (2 teaspoons)

Sea salt or kosher salt to taste

1½ cups ready-to-eat fresh or frozen shelled edamame, thawed

2 cups boiling water

1½ pints cherry, grape and/or pear tomatoes

1 packed cup fresh mint leaves, coarsely chopped

6 thin green onions, thinly sliced

1½ teaspoons fresh lemon zest

Juice of ½ lemon, or to taste

1 cup crumbled feta cheese or soy feta cheese

Tender lettuce leaves, such as Bibb, rinsed and dried

Oil-cured olives, for garnish, optional

1 Combine couscous, 1 tablespoon oil, jalapeños, cumin, coriander, garlic and salt to taste in large bowl; whisk together until couscous is evenly coated. Scatter edamame on top, and pour on boiling water. Cover bowl with plastic wrap. Let stand 5 minutes, until water is absorbed. Uncover bowl, fluff mixture with fork and cool completely.

2 Meanwhile, quarter large and halve small tomatoes, and put in large bowl. Add mint, green onions and lemon zest.

3 Add cooled couscous mixture to tomato mixture with remaining 3 tablespoons oil, lemon juice, or to taste, and salt to taste; toss to combine. Add feta, and gently toss to combine.

4 Line 6 plates with lettuce leaves, and top with salad. Garnish with olives, if using, and serve.

Per Serving: 410 cal; 17g prot; 18g total fat (6g sat. fat); 46g carb; 25mg chol; 380mg sod; 9g fiber; 4g sugars

Mediterranean Couscous and Lentil Salad

SERVES 6

Firm, earthy-tasting French green lentils hold their own in this salad.

15 minutes   30 minutes   45 minutes

1 cup (16 ounces) French green lentils, picked over and rinsed

3 tablespoons white wine vinegar, divided

Salt to taste

Freshly ground black pepper to taste

1¼ cups boiling water

1 cup uncooked couscous

½ teaspoon salt

3 tablespoons plus 2 teaspoons olive oil, divided

1 clove garlic, minced and mashed to a paste with ¼ teaspoon salt

½ cup finely chopped fresh mint

4 cups arugula leaves, rinsed, dried and chopped

2 cups grape tomatoes, halved

½ cup crumbled feta cheese

1 Bring large pot of water to a boil. Add lentils. Reduce heat, and simmer 15 minutes, or until tender. Drain. Transfer to bowl, and stir in 1 tablespoon vinegar. Season to taste with salt and pepper. Cool, stirring occasionally.

2 Pour boiling water over couscous in large bowl. Stir in salt, cover and let stand 5 minutes. Fluff with fork, and stir in 2 teaspoons oil. Cool.

3 Whisk together garlic paste, remaining 3 tablespoons oil, remaining 2 tablespoons vinegar and mint in small bowl. Stir dressing and lentils into couscous.

4 Just before serving, add arugula, tomatoes and feta.

Per Serving: 257 cal; 11g prot; 8g total fat (2g sat. fat); 35g carb; 6mg chol; 309mg sod; 10g fiber; 3g sugars

Grilled Sweet Potato Salad

SERVES 4   VEGAN

Grilled sweet potatoes require close attention—but the results are worth it. Slice them too thick, and they won't cook through; slice them too thin, and they'll char quickly. So slice carefully, and keep an eye on the grill.

15 minutes | 30 minutes | **45** minutes

CILANTRO-LIME VINAIGRETTE

3 tablespoons fresh lime juice

1 tablespoon white wine vinegar

1 teaspoon grated or minced lime zest

¼ cup extra virgin olive oil

2 tablespoons chopped fresh cilantro

2 cloves garlic, minced (2 teaspoons)

Salt to taste

SWEET POTATOES

2 pounds sweet potatoes, peeled and
   sliced ⅜-inch thick

1 red bell pepper, diced

2 green onions, white and tender
   green parts, sliced

3 tablespoons fresh orange, mango
   or pineapple juice

Salt to taste

Freshly ground black pepper to taste

1 Prepare medium-low charcoal fire, or preheat gas grill (or broiler).

2 *To make Cilantro-Lime Vinaigrette:* Combine lime juice, vinegar and zest in large bowl. Whisk in oil until completely blended. Stir in cilantro, garlic and salt.

3 *To make Sweet Potatoes:* Add potato slices to vinaigrette, and let marinate a few minutes. Using slotted spoon, transfer potato slices to grill. Turn occasionally, basting with remaining vinaigrette, and cook until tender when pierced with fork, 10 to 15 minutes.

4 Return grilled potatoes to bowl with vinaigrette. Add red pepper, green onions, juice, salt and pepper; toss gently. Serve immediately.

Per Serving: 270 cal; 3g prot; 14g total fat (2g sat. fat); 34g carb; 0mg chol; 55mg sod; 6g fiber; 13g sugars

Summer Pasta Salad with Grilled Vegetables

SERVES 8   VEGAN

Timing is the only trick here, since the tomatoes and green onions take
less time to cook than the zucchini and peppers.

15 minutes | 30 minutes | **45 minutes**

8 ounces dried rotini, shells or other
short pasta

3 tablespoons extra-virgin olive oil,
divided

2 tablespoons red wine vinegar

2 cloves garlic, minced (2 teaspoons)

Salt to taste

Freshly ground black pepper to taste

1 cup cherry tomatoes

2 medium-sized zucchini, cut
lengthwise into quarters

1 red bell pepper, quartered

1 bunch (4 ounces) green onions,
trimmed

1 cup black brine-cured olives,
such as kalamata

2 tablespoons chopped fresh oregano

2 tablespoons chopped fresh basil

1 Prepare medium-hot charcoal fire, or preheat
gas grill (or broiler). Cover 4 wooden skewers
with water; set aside.

2 Bring large pot of lightly salted water to a boil.
Add pasta, and cook until al dente. Drain, and
rinse thoroughly to cool. Transfer to large bowl,
and toss with 1 tablespoon oil.

3 Whisk together remaining 2 tablespoons oil,
vinegar, garlic, salt and pepper in 9 × 13-inch
baking dish. Add tomatoes, zucchini, red pepper
and green onions, and toss to coat with oil
mixture. Thread cherry tomatoes onto soaked
wooden skewers.

4 Transfer zucchini and red pepper to grill rack.
Grill, turning occasionally, about 3 minutes.
Add tomato skewers and green onions to grill
rack, and cook until all vegetables are tender and
grill-marked, 2 to 4 minutes more. Remove from
grill, and let stand until cool enough to handle.

5 Chop zucchini, red pepper and green onions
coarsely, and add to pasta. Slide tomatoes off
skewers into bowl. Add remaining marinade,
olives and herbs, and toss well.

Per Serving: 190 cal; 5g prot; 8g total fat (1g sat. fat);
28g carb; 0mg chol; 160mg sod; 3g fiber; 3g sugars

5

Soups and Stews

Easy Black Bean Chili

SERVES 4 TO 6   VEGAN

This recipe takes only a few minutes to throw together. Using a good-quality salsa is what makes it so delicious. Serve it topped with shredded Monterey Jack cheese and minced sweet onion, if desired.

15 minutes | 30 minutes | 45 minutes

Two 15-ounce cans black beans, drained and rinsed

One 16-ounce jar roasted garlic salsa

1 bunch (4 ounces) green onions, chopped (white and pale green parts)

One 10-ounce package super-sweet frozen corn kernels

½ cup chopped fresh cilantro

Salt to taste

1 Combine beans, salsa and green onions in large saucepan. Cover, and cook over medium heat, stirring occasionally, 10 minutes.

2 Stir in corn, cilantro and salt to taste, and cook, stirring occasionally, until heated through. Serve hot.

Per Serving: 309 cal; 18g prot; 1g total fat (<1g sat. fat); 60g carb; 0mg chol; 336mg sod; 17g fiber; 3g sugars

Black Bean Soup with Roasted Red Pepper

SERVES 8   VEGAN

A pressure cooker can produce a luscious black bean soup from scratch in under an hour because there is no need to pre-soak the beans. Use 1 or 2 jalapeños depending on how spicy you want your soup.

15 minutes | 30 minutes | **45** minutes

2 tablespoons olive oil, divided

1 medium-sized yellow onion, chopped (about 1½ cups)

2 teaspoons whole cumin seeds

2½ cups (1 pound) dried black beans, picked over and rinsed

2 large cloves garlic

1¼ teaspoons salt, divided

2 large red bell peppers, halved

1 teaspoon Dijon mustard

⅓ cup chopped fresh cilantro

2 tablespoons fresh lime juice

1 to 2 jalapeños chiles, diced

Zest of 1 orange

1 Heat 1 tablespoon oil in 6-quart pressure cooker over medium-high heat. Add onion and cumin, and sauté 3 minutes, or until onion softens. Add 7 cups water, beans, garlic and 1 teaspoon salt.

2 Lock pressure cooker lid in place. Bring to high pressure. Reduce heat, and cook at high pressure 25 minutes. Remove from heat, and allow pressure to come down naturally before removing lid. (If beans are not tender, cover, and simmer over medium-low heat until fully cooked.)

3 Meanwhile, preheat broiler. Roast bell pepper halves skin side up on baking sheet 15 minutes, or until skin is charred. Wrap in wet paper towels until cool enough to handle. Rub off skins. Coarsely chop one pepper, and purée it with mustard, remaining 1 tablespoon oil and remaining ¼ teaspoon salt in mini-chopper or blender. Cut remaining pepper into ½-inch dice.

4 Stir diced red pepper, cilantro, lime juice, jalapeños and orange zest into soup. Ladle into bowls. Spoon 1 tablespoon red pepper purée in center, and swirl. Serve immediately.

Per Serving: 258 cal; 13g prot; 4.5g total fat (0.5g sat. fat); 43g carb; 0mg chol; 448mg sod; 10g fiber; 4g sugars

White Bean Soup with Collard Greens

SERVES 4 VEGAN

Great Northern beans blended with lightly browned onions and nutritious collard greens make this soup delicious, hearty and satisfying. Serve it with whole-grain sourdough bread.

15 minutes 30 minutes **45** minutes

2 tablespoons olive oil

2 cups chopped yellow onions

3 cups finely chopped collard greens, tough stems removed, rinsed and dried

1 teaspoon dried tarragon

³/₄ teaspoon salt

Two 15-ounce cans Great Northern beans, drained and rinsed

Freshly ground black pepper to taste

1 Heat oil in large stockpot over medium heat. Add onions and cook, stirring often, until lightly browned, about 7 minutes.

2 Add collard greens, tarragon, salt and 2 cups water. Bring to a boil, reduce heat to low, cover and cook 20 minutes, or until greens are tender.

3 Meanwhile, put 1 can beans and 1 cup water in food processor or blender, and process until puréed. Add purée and remaining can of beans to stockpot. Cook over medium-low heat, stirring occasionally, until heated through. Season to taste with freshly ground black pepper, and serve hot.

Per Serving: 320 cal; 16g prot; 8g total fat (1g sat. fat); 49g carb; 0mg chol; 450mg sod; 12g fiber; 4g sugars

Three-Bean Soup

SERVES 6

VEGAN

Here's a straight-from-the-pantry soup that'll become a weeknight favorite. Puréeing one of the cans of beans creates a creamy base without adding extra fat or cholesterol. Garnish with crumbled feta cheese and serve with vegetable chips, if desired.

15 minutes **30 minutes** 45 minutes

2 tablespoons vegetable oil

1 large yellow onion, diced (about 2 cups)

One 15.5-ounce can navy beans, drained and rinsed

One 15.5-ounce can black beans, drained and rinsed

6 cloves garlic, minced (2 tablespoons)

2 cups low-sodium vegetable stock or water, divided

One 15.5-ounce can Great Northern beans, drained and rinsed

Salt to taste

Freshly ground black pepper to taste

1 Heat oil in large stockpot over medium heat. Sauté onion 2 to 3 minutes, or until soft. Add navy beans, black beans and garlic, and continue cooking and stirring 8 to 10 minutes more. Stir in 1 cup stock.

2 Meanwhile, put Great Northern beans and remaining 1 cup stock into food processor or blender, and purée until smooth. Pour purée into soup, and stir to blend. Season to taste with salt and pepper. Thin with more stock or water, if desired.

3 Spoon into individual soup bowls, and serve hot.

Per Serving: 231 cal; 13g prot; 5g total fat (0g sat. fat); 39g carb; 0mg chol; 557mg sod; 11g fiber; 5g sugars

Risi e Bisi (Rice and Peas) with Pea Pesto

SERVES 5

This Italian dish is similar to risotto but is more soup-like and easier to prepare. The pesto can be made a day ahead of time, and if there is any left over, it is delicious tossed with pasta or boiled potatoes.

 30 minutes

PEA PESTO

1 cup loosely packed fresh basil leaves

½ cup frozen peas, thawed

3 tablespoons olive oil

3 tablespoons grated Parmesan cheese

2 tablespoons pine nuts, toasted

1 clove garlic

½ teaspoon light brown sugar

Salt to taste

Freshly ground black pepper to taste

RISI E BISI

3 cups vegetable stock

One 2-inch piece Parmesan cheese rind

2 tablespoons olive oil

1 small yellow onion, finely chopped (1 cup)

1 cup Arborio rice

2 cloves garlic, minced (2 teaspoons)

¼ cup sherry

1 cup frozen peas, thawed

1 *To make Pea Pesto:* Combine all ingredients except salt and pepper in bowl of food processor, and pulse until smooth. Season to taste with salt and pepper. Set aside.

2 *To make Risi e Bisi:* Heat stock, 2 cups water, and Parmesan rind in medium-sized saucepan over medium heat. Bring to a simmer, and reduce heat to low.

3 Heat oil in medium-sized saucepan over medium heat. Add onion, and cook 5 minutes, or until translucent. Add rice and garlic, and stir 1 minute, making sure grains are evenly coated with oil. Stir in sherry, and cook 1 minute, or until evaporated.

4 Ladle in 1 cup stock mixture, and stir and cook until stock is below level of rice, 3 to 5 minutes. Add another cup of stock, and repeat process. Continue this process until rice is al dente, 15 to 18 minutes. Add peas and remaining stock, discard cheese rind and simmer 2 to 3 minutes more. Check rice grains; they should be tender but not mushy. Ladle into bowls, and serve with pesto on the side.

Per Serving: 364 cal; 8g prot; 17.5g total fat (2.5g sat. fat); 46g carb; 3mg chol; 474mg sod; 5g fiber; 5g sugars

Black-Eyed Pea Stew with Kale, Butternut Squash and Soy "Sausage"

SERVES 5   VEGAN

The small amount of soy "sausage" in this dish gives it just the right amount of smokiness and spice. If you cannot find a chorizo-like soy "sausage," you can substitute soy "bacon." Although this dish is excellent the day you make it, it tastes even better the next day.

15 minutes **30 minutes** 45 minutes

Nonstick cooking spray

3 ounces chorizo-like soy "sausage," removed from casing and crumbled

1 tablespoon olive oil

2 cups butternut squash, cut into ½-inch dice (about ½ small butternut squash)

1 cup diced yellow onion

1 cup diced carrot

2 cloves garlic, minced (2 teaspoons)

2 cups finely chopped collard greens, tough stems removed, rinsed and dried

One 15-ounce can vegetable stock

One 15-ounce can fire-roasted tomatoes

One 15-ounce can black-eyed peas, drained and rinsed

Salt to taste

Freshly ground black pepper to taste

1 Place large stockpot over medium heat, and spray with nonstick cooking spray. Add soy "sausage," and sauté 1 to 2 minutes. Remove from pot, and set aside.

2 Add oil to pot. Add squash, onion and carrot. Cook, stirring occasionally, 5 to 7 minutes, or until onion is translucent. Stir in garlic, and cook 1 minute more. Add greens, stock, tomatoes and 2 cups water, and cover. Bring mixture to a simmer, and reduce heat. Simmer 10 minutes, stirring occasionally, until greens and squash are tender.

3 Add soy "sausage" and peas to pot, and simmer an additional 5 minutes, partially covered. Season to taste with salt and pepper, and serve hot.

Per Serving: 213 cal; 9g prot; 6g total fat (0.5g sat. fat); 35g carb; 0mg chol; 726mg sod; 8g fiber; 9g sugars

Warm Pea Purée with Aged Goat Cheese and Garlic Toasts

SERVES 6

This is simply spring in a bowl—a warm pea purée accented with tangy goat cheese. You can use fresh peas for this, but frozen peas work beautifully (not to mention quickly!). This also makes a great filling for ravioli.

15 minutes **30 minutes** 45 minutes

1 French baguette, sliced diagonally into ¼-inch slices

2 cloves garlic, one whole and one minced

1 tablespoon olive oil

1 tablespoon unsalted butter

2 leeks, light parts only, thinly sliced (1 cup)

⅔ cup vegetable stock

½ teaspoon granulated sugar

2 cups frozen peas

Salt to taste

Freshly ground black pepper to taste

2 ounces aged goat cheese, such as Boucheron or Humboldt Fog

1 Preheat oven to 350°F.

2 Put bread slices on baking sheet, and bake 15 to 17 minutes, or until crisp and golden. Let cool slightly, then rub edges of each crouton with whole garlic clove. Set aside.

3 Heat oil and butter in large nonstick skillet over medium-low heat. Add leeks, and cook 5 to 7 minutes, stirring occasionally. Add minced garlic, and cook 1 minute more. Add stock and sugar, and raise heat to medium. Simmer 3 to 5 minutes, or until liquid is reduced by half.

4 Stir in peas, and cook 2 to 3 minutes, or until they have thawed and turn bright green. Let cool slightly, then purée in food processor until chunky-smooth. Season to taste with salt and pepper.

5 Spoon purée into medium-sized bowl, and crumble goat cheese on top. Serve with garlic toasts.

Per Serving: 235 cal; 9g prot; 8.5g total fat (3.5g sat. fat); 31g carb; 12mg chol; 424mg sod; 5g fiber; 4g sugars

"Cream" of Asparagus Soup

Puréeing an aromatic rice (such as basmati or jasmine) adds delicate flavor and creates a creamy, nondairy soup base when blended with broth and veggies (in this case, asparagus) until smooth. This recipe also works well with 2 pounds of broccoli—just reserve 1 cup of florets to stir in at the end, the same way you would add the asparagus tips.

2 pounds asparagus, woody ends trimmed

2 tablespoons olive oil

3 cups chopped yellow onions

²/₃ cup uncooked basmati or jasmine rice

2 low-sodium vegetable bouillon cubes

2 sprigs fresh thyme

1 Cut asparagus into ½-inch pieces, setting tips aside.

2 Heat oil in large stockpot over medium heat. Add onions, and sauté 5 minutes, or until soft. Stir in asparagus pieces, rice, bouillon cubes, thyme and 8 cups water. Reduce heat, cover and cook 30 to 35 minutes, or until rice is very tender. Remove and discard thyme sprigs.

3 Transfer soup to blender or food processor in 2 batches (or use an immersion blender), and purée until smooth. Return soup to pot, and add asparagus tips. Simmer 1 to 2 minutes over low heat, or until asparagus tips are bright green and crisp-tender. Ladle soup into bowls, and serve immediately.

Per Serving: 117 cal; 4g prot; 4g total fat (0.5g sat. fat); 18g carb; 0mg chol; 25mg sod; 3g fiber; 3g sugars

Pumpkin-Coconut Bisque

SERVES 4   VEGAN

Smooth and mysteriously piquant, this lush soup contains several Asian
seasonings, yet it is at home as part of any American meal. When buying
Thai red curry paste, check the label—some contain fish or shrimp.
Roasting the pumpkin enhances its flavor, but you may omit the step.

15 minutes   30 minutes   **45** minutes

1¾ cups canned pumpkin

2 tablespoons vegetable oil

1 yellow onion, chopped

1 tablespoon shredded peeled
    fresh ginger

½ to 1 teaspoon red curry paste,
    or to taste

1¾ cups light coconut milk, divided

½ cup vegetable stock

6 tablespoons frozen apple juice
    concentrate

Salt to taste

½ cup toasted pumpkin seeds,
    for garnish

1 cup garlic-flavored croutons,
    for garnish

1 Preheat oven to 450°F.

2 To roast pumpkin purée, put purée into
ovenproof dish, and heat until edges brown,
about 15 minutes.

3 Meanwhile, heat oil in large skillet or wok
over medium heat, and sauté onion and ginger
about 10 minutes. Add curry paste; sauté
2 minutes more.

4 Transfer onion mixture and 1 cup roasted
pumpkin purée to blender or food processor;
add 1 cup coconut milk, and purée until
smooth.

5 Pour mixture into large saucepan, and stir in
remaining ¾ cup pumpkin purée, remaining
¾ cup coconut milk, vegetable stock, apple
juice concentrate and salt to taste. Heat 5 minutes. Garnish each serving with sprinkling of
pumpkin seeds and croutons.

Per Serving: 340 cal; 11g prot; 21g total fat (5g sat.
fat); 27g carb; 0mg chol; 260mg sod; 3g fiber;
8g sugars

Steaming Miso Soup with Vegetables

SERVES 4   VEGAN

Talk about instant comfort! A handful of veggies from the salad bar and a few chunks of baked tofu turn a package of miso soup mix into a soul-satisfying meal. Just make sure the soup brand you buy contains no fish ingredients (often listed as powdered bonito or bonito flakes).

15 minutes 30 minutes 45 minutes

Half of 0.7-ounce package instant miso soup, with or without seaweed

1 cup broccoli florets

¼ cup sliced white button mushrooms

2 slices peeled fresh ginger, optional

20 fresh baby spinach leaves, rinsed and dried

2 ounces baked Oriental-style tofu, cubed

Combine soup mix, 1½ cups water, broccoli, mushrooms and ginger, if using, in medium-sized microwave-safe bowl. Heat on high 3 minutes. Add spinach and tofu, and microwave 30 seconds more. Discard ginger slices before eating. Serve hot.

Per Serving: 156 cal; 15g prot; 6.5g total fat (1g sat. fat); 11g carb; 0mg chol; 1,120mg sod; 7g fiber; 2g sugars

Broccoli-Shirataki Noodle Soup

SERVES 2   VEGAN

This Vietnamese-style soup is made in the microwave using a single bowl.
Shirataki noodles have only 20 calories per serving and can be found in
the refrigerated tofu section of Asian groceries and large supermarkets.

2 large limes

1½ cups low-sodium vegetable broth

6 green onions, divided

4 stems cilantro, divided

1 1-inch piece fresh ginger, sliced

2 cloves garlic, peeled and crushed

¾ cup sliced mushrooms

¾ cup baby carrots, halved

½ red bell pepper, chopped
   (about ½ cup)

1 8-oz. bag fettucine-style tofu shirataki
   noodles, rinsed

2 cups broccoli florets (about 6 oz.)

¼ tsp. chili sauce, such as Sriracha,
   optional

1 Zest one lime with vegetable peeler. Combine
zest, broth and 1½ cups water in large microwave-
safe bowl. Coarsely chop 4 green onions, and
add to liquid along with 3 stems cilantro, ginger
and garlic. Cover tightly with plastic wrap,
and heat in the microwave on high power
10 minutes. Let stand 1 minute. Remove plastic
wrap, and strain broth, discarding onion-cilantro
mixture.

2 Return broth to bowl, and add mushrooms,
carrots and bell pepper. Cover with plastic wrap,
and heat on high power 5 minutes. Let stand
1 minute.

3 Cut noodles into shorter strands with scissors.
Add noodles to broth, and top with broccoli.
Cover, and heat 3 minutes or more. Chop
remaining 2 green onions, and pluck sprigs
from remaining cilantro stem. Cut remaining
lime into wedges. Stir chopped green onions
and chili sauce, if desired, into soup. Ladle
into bowls, and garnish with cilantro sprigs
and lime wedges.

Per Serving: 102 cal; 5g prot; 1g total fat (0g sat. fat);
22g carb; 0mg chol; 345mg sod; 7g fiber; 6g sugars

Carrot Soup with Asparagus and Pastina

SERVES 4 · VEGAN

Coriander really helps bring out the sweetness of the carrot juice in this pretty orange soup. If you cannot find pastina, substitute any small pasta, such as orzo.

15 minutes | **30 minutes** | 45 minutes

½ cup dried pastina or orzo

2 tablespoons olive oil

1 medium-sized yellow onion, finely chopped

1 small carrot, cut into ¼-inch dice

2 cloves garlic, minced (2 teaspoons)

¼ teaspoon ground coriander

1 tablespoon sherry

2 cups vegetable stock

2 cups carrot juice

4 ounces asparagus, ends trimmed and cut into ¼-inch-thick rounds (1 cup)

1 teaspoon sherry vinegar

Salt to taste

Freshly ground black pepper to taste

1 Cook pasta according to package directions; rinse with cold water, and drain. Set aside.

2 Heat oil in medium-sized pot over medium heat. Add onion and carrot, and sauté 7 to 9 minutes, or until carrots are crisp-tender. Stir in garlic and coriander, and cook 1 minute. Add sherry, and stir 1 minute. Add stock and carrot juice. Bring to a simmer, and cook 5 minutes, or until carrots are tender. Add asparagus, and cook 2 to 3 minutes more, or until asparagus is crisp-tender. Stir in sherry vinegar and pasta. Season to taste with salt and pepper, and serve hot.

Per Serving: 213 cal; 5g prot; 7g total fat (1g sat. fat); 32g carb; 0mg chol; 430mg sod; 2g fiber; 5g sugars

Curried Spinach-Potato Soup

SERVES 4

This soup packs in a lot of flavor as well as a lot of lutein, which helps keep eyes healthy. It will become a favorite recipe because it goes together fast.

1 tablespoon olive oil

1 cup chopped leeks, white and light green parts

1 tablespoon curry powder, or to taste

2½ cups vegetable stock

2 small white potatoes, peeled and cut into ½-inch pieces (about 1½ cups)

1 teaspoon salt

4 packed cups fresh baby spinach leaves, rinsed and dried

2 cups 1 percent milk

Freshly ground black pepper to taste

Plain nonfat yogurt, for garnish, optional

1 Heat oil in large saucepan over medium heat. Add leeks and 1 tablespoon water, and cook, stirring often, until tender, about 5 minutes. Add curry powder, and stir 30 seconds. Add stock, potatoes and salt, and bring to a boil. Reduce heat to low, cover and cook until potatoes are tender, about 10 minutes. Stir in spinach, and cook until just wilted, about 1 minute. Cool slightly.

2 Transfer soup to blender, and blend until almost smooth; work in batches if necessary.

3 Return soup to saucepan. Add milk, and cook over medium-low heat. Season to taste with salt and pepper.

4 Ladle soup into 4 bowls. Garnish with swirl of yogurt, if using, and serve.

Per Serving: 160 cal; 6g prot; 5g total fat (1.5g sat. fat); 25g carb; 5mg chol; 930mg sod; 3g fiber; 8g sugars

Cauliflower and Leek Potage

SERVES 6   VEGAN

This nondairy creamy soup is very easy to make if you have a handheld immersion blender, which allows you to purée the ingredients right in the pot. *Herbes de Provence* adds a medley of dried-herb flavors in a dash.

<del>15 minutes</del> **30** minutes <del>45 minutes</del>

1 head (3 pounds) cauliflower, trimmed and chopped

2 medium-sized leeks, trimmed and chopped

3 cups vegetable stock

2 teaspoons *herbes de Provence*

2 cups plain soymilk

Salt to taste

Freshly ground black pepper to taste

1 Combine cauliflower, leeks, stock and *herbes de Provence* in large saucepan. Bring to a boil. Reduce heat to low, cover and cook, stirring occasionally, about 15 minutes.

2 Remove from heat, and stir in soymilk. Purée soup with immersion blender, or transfer to food processor and purée, adding more soymilk if needed for desired consistency. Return soup to pot (if using a food processor), stir in salt and pepper to taste and reheat over low heat. Serve hot.

Per Serving: 110 cal; 7g prot; 2g total fat (0g sat. fat); 18g carb; 0mg chol; 270mg sod; 6g fiber; 7g sugars

Mediterranean Eggplant and Fennel Stew

SERVES 6   VEGAN

A few pulses of the immersion blender thickens this hearty stew without turning it into soup. If you can find them, use organic fire-roasted tomatoes to achieve particularly tasty results.

15 minutes   **30** minutes   45 minutes

1 bulb fresh fennel

1 tablespoon olive oil

1 large yellow onion, chopped

2 cloves garlic, minced (2 teaspoons)

One 28-ounce can diced tomatoes

1½ cups low-sodium vegetable stock

2 medium-sized eggplants (about 1½ pounds), peeled and cut into 1-inch cubes

⅓ cup pitted, chopped kalamata olives

¼ teaspoon ground cinnamon

1 bay leaf

2 tablespoons minced capers

2 teaspoons balsamic vinegar

1 Trim fennel stalks and fronds. Finely chop fronds, and reserve for garnish. Quarter fennel bulb lengthwise. Remove and discard any outer fibrous layers, and trim core. Cut each quarter crosswise into ¼-inch-thick slices. Set aside.

2 Heat oil in 6-quart Dutch oven over medium-high heat. Add onion and garlic, and cook 3 to 5 minutes, or until onion is lightly browned, stirring often. Add fennel, tomatoes, stock, eggplants, olives, cinnamon and bay leaf.

3 Bring mixture to a boil. Reduce heat to medium-low, cover and cook 15 minutes, or until eggplant and fennel are tender, stirring occasionally. Remove and discard bay leaf. Submerge immersion blender deep into mixture to avoid splattering, and purée just enough to thicken stew. Stir in capers and vinegar. Serve hot, sprinkling each serving with fennel fronds.

Per Serving: 128 cal; 4g prot; 3.5g total fat (0.5g sat. fat); 21g carb; 0mg chol; 707mg sod; 6g fiber; 10g sugars

Lemony Lentil–Spinach Stew

SERVES 4   VEGAN

Fresh mint turns this simple stew into a knockout one-pot dinner.

15 minutes 30 minutes **45 minutes**

2 teaspoons olive oil

2 cloves garlic, minced (2 teaspoons)

3 cups low-sodium vegetable stock

1 cup (16 ounces) brown lentils, picked over and rinsed

3 medium-sized red-skinned potatoes, cut into ½-inch dice (about ½ pound)

6 ounces (3½ cups) fresh baby spinach leaves, rinsed and dried

2 tablespoons fresh lemon juice

½ teaspoon lemon zest

¼ teaspoon cayenne

¼ cup chopped fresh mint

Salt to taste

Freshly ground black pepper to taste

1 Heat oil in saucepan over medium heat. Add garlic, and cook 30 seconds. Add stock and lentils, and bring to a boil. Reduce heat, cover and simmer 10 minutes. Add potatoes, and cook 15 minutes, or until lentils are tender.

2 Add spinach, lemon juice, lemon zest and cayenne. Cover, and simmer 2 minutes, or until spinach wilts. Stir in mint. Season to taste with salt and pepper. Serve hot.

Per Serving: 276 cal; 18g prot; 3.5g total fat (0.5g sat. fat); 46g carb; 0mg chol; 456mg sod; 20g fiber; 6g sugars

Tuscan Vegetable Ragoût

SERVES 4   VEGAN

For a heartier dish, add diced and browned tofu or seitan near the end of the cooking time. This delicious mélange is especially good accompanied by crusty Italian bread or served over pasta.

15 minutes 30 minutes **45 minutes**

2 teaspoons olive oil

2 zucchini, halved lengthwise and cut into ½-inch slices

3 cloves garlic, minced (1 tablespoon)

Two 15.5-ounce cans cannellini beans, drained and rinsed

One 15-ounce can artichoke hearts, quartered

One 8-ounce can diced tomatoes, undrained

¼ cup chopped fresh parsley or basil, divided

2 tablespoons coarsely chopped kalamata olives

1 tablespoon capers, coarsely chopped

Salt to taste

Freshly ground black pepper to taste

1 Heat oil in large stockpot over medium heat. Add zucchini and garlic, cover and cook until softened, about 5 minutes. Stir in beans, artichoke hearts and tomatoes, and cook until vegetables are tender, about 15 minutes.

2 Add ⅛ cup parsley, olives and capers, and stir to blend. Season to taste with salt and pepper. Serve sprinkled with remaining parsley.

Per Serving: 380 cal; 23g prot; 4.5g total fat (0.5g sat. fat); 68g carb; 0mg chol; 1,000mg sod; 20g fiber; 8g sugars

6

Side Dishes

Glazed Tofu

SERVES 4 VEGAN

A few minutes of simmering in a luscious maple glaze flavors this firm tofu.
The cubes are wonderful in stir-fries and salads.

| 15 minutes | **30** minutes | 45 minutes |

3 tablespoons maple syrup

3 tablespoons mirin

2 tablespoons low-sodium tamari or
   soy sauce

1 pound firm or extra-firm tofu, drained
   and pressed for 15 minutes

1 tablespoon vegetable oil

1 Mix maple syrup, mirin and tamari in small
bowl. Set aside.

2 Cut tofu into ¾-inch cubes. Heat oil in
nonstick skillet over medium-high heat. Add
tofu, and fry until golden, about 10 minutes,
turning every 3 minutes. (You don't need to
brown all 6 sides.) Add syrup mixture, and cook
3 to 4 minutes, turning occasionally, until tofu is
coated with glaze. Serve hot.

Per Serving: 200 cal; 14g prot; 11g total fat (1.5g
sat. fat); 12g carb; 0mg chol; 520mg sod; 1g fiber;
9g sugars

Mardi Gras Slaw

SERVES 8

The Mardi Gras colors are purple, green and gold, and this salad celebrates the season. Another plus: It doesn't wilt on a buffet table.

15 minutes 30 minutes 45 minutes

SLAW

1 small head (2½ lbs) green cabbage, halved and cored

½ head (1½ lbs) red cabbage, cored

3 yellow bell peppers

BLUE CHEESE DRESSING

½ cup olive oil

2½ to 3 tablespoons white wine vinegar

1 clove garlic, minced (1 teaspoon)

½ teaspoon salt

½ teaspoon freshly ground black pepper

2 ounces blue cheese, crumbled

1 *To make Slaw:* Slice cabbages into fine shreds. Put in large bowl. Slice peppers very thinly lengthwise, and add to bowl.

2 *To make Blue Cheese Dressing:* Put all the ingredients in quart jar, screw on lid and shake vigorously. Pour half over slaw, and toss. Refrigerate remainder for up to 7 days for future use.

Per Serving: 200 cal; 4g prot; 16g total fat (3g sat. fat); 12g carb; 5mg chol; 280mg sod; 4g fiber; 6g sugars

Potatoes *Tarka* (Potatoes with Cumin Seeds)

SERVES 4   VEGAN

This simple Indian recipe transforms boiled potatoes. If the cumin seeds cook too long and burn (they will look black and lose their fragrance), just start over with fresh oil and seeds before adding the potatoes.

1 pound new potatoes, quartered

2 tablespoons vegetable oil

1 tablespoon cumin seeds

½ teaspoon salt

¼ teaspoon freshly ground black pepper

1 Put potatoes in large saucepan with enough salted water to cover. Bring to a boil; reduce heat, and simmer 5 minutes, or until potatoes are tender. Drain well.

2 Heat oil in large nonstick skillet over medium-high heat. Add cumin seeds, and cook 15 seconds, or until fragrant and brown. Stir in potatoes, salt and pepper. Adjust seasonings to taste, and serve immediately.

Per Serving: 163 cal; 2.5g prot; 7g total fat (0.5g sat. fat); 23g carb; 0mg chol; 371mg sod; 2g fiber; 0g sugars

Masala Potatoes with Peas and Cilantro

SERVES 4   VEGAN

This dish was inspired by the southern Indian dish *masala dosa*—a burrito-like dish filled with seasoned potatoes. The potatoes are colored a golden yellow from the turmeric and are subtly seasoned with ginger and mustard seed. Serve this with flour tortillas.

15 minutes | **30 minutes** | 45 minutes

2 large russet potatoes (about 1½ pounds), peeled and sliced into ¼-inch rounds

2 tablespoons canola oil

1½ teaspoons black mustard seeds

½ teaspoon cumin seeds

1 medium-sized onion, diced (1½ cups)

1 jalapeño chile, seeded and diced

2 cloves garlic, minced (2 teaspoons)

½ teaspoon grated peeled fresh ginger

½ teaspoon ground turmeric

½ teaspoon curry powder

1 cup frozen peas, thawed

¼ cup chopped fresh cilantro

Salt to taste

Freshly ground black pepper to taste

1 Put potatoes in large pot with enough salted water to cover by 1 inch. Place over high heat, and bring to a boil. Reduce heat to medium, and simmer potatoes 7 to 9 minutes, or until tender. Drain and set aside.

2 Heat oil in large nonstick skillet over medium heat; add mustard and cumin seeds. Stir 2 to 3 minutes, or until mustard seeds start to pop. Add onion and jalapeño, and stir 5 to 7 minutes, or until onion is translucent. Add garlic, ginger, turmeric, and curry, and cook for 2 minutes more, stirring occasionally.

3 Reduce heat to low, and add drained potatoes and ½ cup water. Stir to combine potatoes with seasonings. Add peas and cilantro, and stir gently to combine—you want a chunky mixture in the end. Season to taste with salt and pepper.

Per Serving: 262 cal; 6g prot; 8g total fat (0.5g sat. fat); 44g carb; 0mg chol; 509mg sod; 6g fiber; 6g sugars

Red Potatoes with Kale, Avocado and Feta

SERVES 4

Combining the hot greens and potatoes with avocados and feta, which softens and melts slightly, gives this simple recipe a striking mix of textures.

15 minutes 30 minutes **45** minutes

8 cups finely chopped kale, rinsed and dried

4 medium-sized red potatoes (1¾ pounds), cut into 1½-inch chunks

1 cup crumbled feta cheese

1 large or 2 small Hass avocados, peeled and diced

2 tablespoons balsamic vinegar

Freshly ground black pepper to taste

1 Put kale in large, heavy pot. Arrange potato chunks on top of kale, and add 1 cup water. Cover, and bring to a boil. Reduce heat to low, and cook until kale is tender, 15 to 20 minutes. Check about halfway through; add a little water if necessary to keep vegetables from burning.

2 Using slotted spoon, transfer vegetables to large bowl. Crumble feta over potatoes and kale. Top with avocado, sprinkle with balsamic vinegar and season to taste with pepper. Serve hot.

Per Serving: 400 cal; 13g prot; 17g total fat (8g sat. fat); 50g carb; 40mg chol; 520mg sod; 8g fiber; 7g sugars

Garlicky Braised Greens
with Balsamic Vinegar and Capers

SERVES 6   VEGAN

When you regularly eat mineral-rich dark leafy greens such as kale and collards, every cell in your body thanks you.

15 minutes | **30** minutes | 45 minutes

10 cloves garlic, peeled

¼ cup extra virgin olive oil

3 tablespoons capers, drained

2 pounds greens, rinsed, dried, stemmed and cut into 1-inch pieces

1 teaspoon salt

Freshly ground black pepper to taste

2 teaspoons balsamic vinegar

1 Crush each garlic clove with flat blade of heavy knife, and slice each crushed clove in half.

2 Heat oil in large pot over medium heat. Add garlic, and cook 2 to 3 minutes, stirring often, or until garlic starts to brown. Add capers, and cook, tossing, 1 minute more. Add greens, salt, pepper and 1 cup water. Toss greens with tongs, pushing uncooked leaves to bottom, until all greens are wilted. Reduce heat to low, and cook, covered, about 10 minutes, or until greens are tender.

3 Uncover, increase heat to high and cook, stirring often, until almost all liquid has evaporated, 2 to 3 minutes. Remove from heat, and stir in vinegar. Serve hot.

Per Serving: 70 cal; 2g prot; 5g total fat (0.5g sat. fat); 6g carb; 0mg chol; 270mg sod; 1g fiber; 0g sugars

Garlicky Brussels Sprout Sauté

SERVES 6   VEGAN

Even people who don't like Brussels sprouts will eat—and enjoy—this fast dish with a tender crunch. Pre-peeled garlic cloves from the produce section make this recipe even quicker.

15 minutes | **30 minutes** | 45 minutes

1 pound Brussels sprouts, ends
  trimmed

2 tablespoons olive oil

12 cloves garlic, peeled and quartered
  lengthwise

1 tablespoon brown sugar

½ teaspoon salt

⅛ teaspoon freshly ground black
  pepper

1 tablespoon apple cider vinegar

1 Put Brussels sprouts in bowl of food processor. Pulse 12 to 15 times, or until shredded.

2 Heat oil in large nonstick skillet over medium-low heat. Add garlic, and cook 5 to 7 minutes, or until light brown. Increase heat to medium-high, and add shredded Brussels sprouts, brown sugar, salt and pepper. Cook 5 minutes, or until browned, stirring often. Add 1½ cups water, and cook 5 minutes more, or until most of liquid is evaporated. Stir in vinegar, and season to taste with salt and pepper. Serve immediately.

Per Serving: 87 cal; 3g prot; 4.5g total fat (0.5g sat. fat); 10g carb; 0mg chol; 213mg sod; 3g fiber; 2g sugars

Edamame Succotash

SERVES 6

VEGAN

Green soybeans, called edamame, have a sweet, nutty flavor. Standing in for the traditional lima beans, they offer a great variation on this classic dish. Edamame are available frozen and fresh, in the pod and shelled. Look for them in large supermarkets, natural-food stores or Asian markets. For a great twist, serve the succotash in hollowed-out tomatoes. If you're using frozen edamame, prepare them first according to package directions, omitting any salt, and drain well.

15 minutes   30 minutes   45 minutes

2 teaspoons vegetable oil

½ cup chopped red bell pepper

¼ cup chopped yellow onion

2 cloves garlic, minced (2 teaspoons)

2 cups fresh or frozen corn kernels

1½ cups fresh or frozen shelled edamame

3 tablespoons white wine or vegetable stock

2 tablespoons chopped fresh parsley

1 tablespoon chopped fresh basil, or 1 teaspoon dried basil

½ teaspoon salt

¼ teaspoon freshly ground black pepper

1 Heat oil in large nonstick skillet over medium heat. Add bell pepper, onion and garlic, and cook, stirring frequently, 2 minutes. Stir in corn, edamame and wine; cook 4 minutes, stirring frequently.

2 Remove skillet from heat. Stir in parsley, basil, salt and pepper. Serve warm.

Per Serving: 140 cal; 8g prot; 5g total fat (0.5g sat. fat); 18g carb; 0mg chol; 200mg sod; 4g fiber; 3g sugars

Broccoli Rabe with Roasted Tomatoes

SERVES 6   VEGAN

Italians love broccoli rabe, a relative of both turnips and cabbage. Cherry tomatoes are a great choice for summer-sweet flavor after tomatoes go out of season. Here, they tame assertive broccoli rabe, making for a colorful and harmonious match.

15 minutes 30 minutes **45 minutes**

1 pint cherry tomatoes

4 tablespoons olive oil, preferably extra-virgin, divided

1 tablespoon balsamic vinegar

½ teaspoon salt

⅛ teaspoon freshly ground black pepper

5 cloves garlic: 3 thinly sliced, 2 minced

4 sprigs fresh rosemary

1 large bunch (about 1 pound) broccoli rabe, large stems removed

1 Preheat oven to 375°F.

2 Spread tomatoes in an 8 × 8-inch glass baking dish. Toss with 3 tablespoons olive oil, vinegar, salt, black pepper and sliced garlic. Tuck rosemary sprigs among tomatoes. Roast uncovered, 30 minutes, or until tomatoes are wrinkled. Discard rosemary.

3 Heat remaining 1 tablespoon olive oil in large skillet over medium heat. Cook minced garlic 1 to 2 minutes, or until golden. Add broccoli rabe. Cover, reduce heat to medium-low and cook 3 to 5 minutes, or until tender. Uncover, and stir in tomatoes. Season to taste with salt and pepper. Serve hot.

Per Serving: 115 cal; 2g prot; 9.5g total fat (1g sat. fat); 7g carb; 0mg chol; 216mg sod; 2g fiber; 2g sugars

Blistered Cherry Tomatoes with Marjoram, Garlic and Ricotta Salata

SERVES 4

This is the perfect preparation for less-than-perfect tomatoes. Cooking them over high heat helps to bring out their flavor and concentrate their sugars. Try this tossed with pasta for a quick and delicious meal.

15 minutes 30 minutes 45 minutes

3 cups cherry tomatoes (1 pound)

1 tablespoon olive oil

½ teaspoon granulated sugar

1 tablespoon chopped fresh marjoram

1 clove garlic, minced (1 teaspoon)

Salt to taste

Freshly ground black pepper to taste

2 ounces ricotta salata cheese, grated (¼ cup)

1 Place large cast-iron skillet over high heat. When pan is very hot, add tomatoes, oil and sugar. Cook, stirring occasionally, 4 to 5 minutes, or until tomatoes are blistered and slightly blackened.

2 Remove from heat, and stir in marjoram and garlic. Season to taste with salt and pepper. Spoon into serving dish, and sprinkle cheese over tomatoes.

Per Serving: 104 cal; 4g prot; 8g total fat (3.5g sat. fat); 6g carb; 15mg chol; 326mg sod; 1g fiber; 4g sugars

Sugar Snap Peas Almondine

SERVES 6

Using sugar snap peas makes a traditional almondine side dish come together super-fast, since the peas cook in half the time of green beans and there are no ends to snap off.

15 minutes 30 minutes 45 minutes

2 teaspoons unsalted butter or olive oil

1 clove garlic, minced (1 teaspoon)

2 shallots, chopped

1 pound sugar snap peas

2 tablespoons fresh lemon zest

¾ teaspoon salt, or more to taste

⅛ teaspoon freshly ground black pepper, or more to taste

¼ cup slivered almonds, toasted

2 tablespoons fresh lemon juice

Heat butter in large skillet over medium heat. Cook garlic and shallots 2 to 3 minutes, or until soft. Stir in sugar snap peas, lemon zest, salt and pepper, and cook 3 minutes more, or until peas are tender and bright green. Add almonds and lemon juice, and cook until just heated through. Adjust seasonings if necessary, and serve immediately.

Per Serving: 80 cal; 3g prot; 4.5g total fat (1g sat. fat); 8g carb; 5mg chol; 300mg sod; 3g fiber; 4g sugars

Braised Fennel with Orange Juice and Toasted Hazelnuts

SERVES 4   VEGAN

Braising the fennel bulbs with orange juice and zest helps to bring out the sweet anise flavor of this vegetable. While this makes a great warm side dish, it is also wonderful tossed with wide pasta noodles, green olives and ricotta salata. This dish can be prepared up to 2 days ahead of time.

15 minutes 30 minutes **45 minutes**

Nonstick cooking spray

2 tablespoons olive oil

4 medium-sized fennel bulbs, cored and quartered

½ cup white wine

½ cup vegetable stock

½ cup orange juice

1 teaspoon orange zest

1 clove garlic, smashed

Salt to taste

Freshly ground black pepper to taste

¼ cup toasted hazelnuts, coarsely chopped

1 Preheat oven to 350°F. Spray 9 × 9-inch baking dish with cooking spray.

2 Heat oil in large skillet over medium-high heat. Add fennel, and cook 2 to 3 minutes on each side, or until browned. Add wine, and cook 2 minutes more, or until wine evaporates. Add stock, juice, zest and garlic, and bring to a simmer. Season to taste with salt and pepper.

3 Remove fennel from skillet, and place in baking dish. Pour remaining liquid over fennel, and cover dish with aluminum foil. Bake 20 minutes, or until fennel is tender.

4 Place fennel in serving dish. Transfer liquid back to skillet, place over medium-high heat and cook for 5 to 7 minutes, or until reduced to about ¾ cup. Pour sauce over fennel, and sprinkle hazelnuts on top.

Per Serving: 199 cal; 4g prot; 11.5g total fat (1g sat. fat); 23g carb; 0mg chol; 319mg sod; 8g fiber; 4g sugars

Roasted Cauliflower with Olives

SERVES 6

VEGAN

A few roasted olives give golden-brown cauliflower florets a rich, salty tang. If you have any leftovers of this rustic side dish (unlikely!), add them to salads, or mash and spread them on crusty bread.

15 minutes 30 minutes **45** minutes

1 medium-sized head (about 1½ pounds) cauliflower, cut into florets

2 tablespoons olive oil

½ teaspoon salt

⅛ teaspoon freshly ground black pepper

¼ cup pitted kalamata olives, quartered

¼ cup chopped fresh parsley

1 Preheat oven to 375°F.

2 Toss cauliflower with olive oil, salt and pepper. Spread florets on baking sheet, and roast 30 minutes, or until cauliflower begins to brown, stirring halfway through. Add olives, and roast 10 minutes more, or until cauliflower is golden and olives begin to shrivel.

3 Sprinkle with chopped parsley, and serve immediately.

Per Serving: 78 cal; 3g prot; 4.5g total fat (0.5g sat. fat); 8g carb; 0mg chol; 411mg sod; 4g fiber; 4g sugars

Curried Corn with Chiles

SERVES 6   VEGAN

Crossing India with Mexico may seem like an odd culinary concept, but this curry is incredibly sweet, fragrant and packed with flavor. Fresh white corn is ideal, but frozen kernels will work too. Serve this with basmati rice and chutney.

15 minutes **30 minutes** 45 minutes

2 tablespoons vegetable oil

1 bunch (4 ounces) green onions, minced

1½ 14-ounce cans light coconut milk, divided

1½ tablespoons ground coriander, or to taste

2 teaspoons ground cumin, or to taste

2 teaspoons curry powder, or to taste

Generous pinch cayenne

Grated zest of 1 lemon

4 cups corn kernels

Salt to taste

2 large poblano chiles, roasted, peeled, seeded and diced

¼ cup chopped fresh cilantro leaves, for garnish

1 Heat oil in large saucepan over medium heat, and sauté green onions 2 to 3 minutes. Stir in ½ cup coconut milk, coriander, cumin, curry and cayenne; cook 3 minutes, stirring often.

2 Add remaining coconut milk and lemon zest, and cook 2 to 3 minutes. Stir in corn kernels and salt to taste, and cook 3 to 4 minutes, or until heated through. Stir in chiles, and cook 1 minute more. Garnish with cilantro, and serve hot.

Per Serving: 260 cal; 7g prot; 13g total fat (6g sat. fat); 33g carb; 0mg chol; 40mg sod; 6g fiber; 6g sugars

A Little Stew of Corn and Mushrooms

SERVES 4   VEGAN

Pairing corn with mushrooms yields an earthy side dish that's brightened by a few dashes of Marsala or sherry.

15 minutes **30 minutes** 45 minutes

3 tablespoons olive oil

¼ cup chopped shallots or red onion

¼ cup chopped green onions

1 pound cremini or chanterelle mushrooms, thickly sliced

Salt to taste

Freshly ground black pepper to taste

1½ cups corn kernels

3 tablespoons Marsala or dry sherry

3 tablespoons julienned fresh basil

1 Heat 2 tablespoons oil in large skillet over medium heat. Add shallots and green onions, and sauté until softened, about 3 minutes. Add mushrooms, salt and pepper to taste and remaining 1 tablespoon oil, and continue cooking about 7 minutes, or until mushrooms soften.

2 Add corn kernels and 2 tablespoons Marsala. Increase heat to medium-high, and cook 5 minutes, or until pan juices become syrupy. To serve, drizzle on remaining 1 tablespoon Marsala, and garnish with basil.

Per Serving: 190 cal; 5g prot; 11g total fat (1.5g sat. fat); 19g carb; 0mg chol; 20mg sod; 3g fiber; 5g sugars

Wild Rice with Broccoli Rabe and Gorgonzola

SERVES 4

This colorful entrée incorporates both American wild rice and European flavors, making it truly international.

30 minutes

One 2.75-ounce package instant wild rice

2 tablespoons olive oil

6 ounces broccoli rabe, trimmed and coarsely chopped

1 red bell pepper, thinly sliced

3 cloves garlic, minced (1 tablespoon)

1 teaspoon dried oregano

½ teaspoon crushed red pepper

Salt to taste

Freshly ground black pepper to taste

½ cup crumbled Gorgonzola cheese

1 Cook wild rice according to package directions. Set aside.

2 Meanwhile, heat olive oil in large nonstick skillet over medium heat. Add broccoli rabe and bell pepper, and sauté 3 minutes, or until broccoli rabe starts to wilt.

3 Stir in garlic, oregano, crushed red pepper and wild rice, and sauté 5 minutes more, or until pepper strips are soft and dish is heated through. Season to taste with salt and pepper.

4 Spoon onto plates, and sprinkle with cheese.

Per Serving: 214 cal; 8g prot; 12g total fat (4g sat. fat); 21g carb; 13mg chol; 394mg sod; 3g fiber; 1g sugars

Crusted Onion Basmati Rice

SERVES 8   VEGAN

Twice-cooked rice the Persian way: Use a hot saucepan to form a golden crust, known as a *tadiq*, on already cooked rice.

15 minutes | 30 minutes | 45 minutes

SPICE MIXTURE

½ cup hot water

3 tablespoons vegetable oil

2 tablespoons coriander seeds

1 teaspoon ground turmeric

RICE

6 cups cold water

2 cups uncooked basmati rice

1 tablespoon sea salt

1 large sweet onion, such as Vidalia or Maui, cut crosswise into ¼-inch-thick slices

1 *To make Spice Mixture:* Combine all the ingredients in small bowl, and set aside.

2 *To make Rice:* Put water, rice and salt in large saucepan, and bring to a boil over medium-high heat. Cook uncovered 12 minutes, stirring occasionally. Drain rice, and rinse with cold water.

3 Re-heat saucepan over medium-high heat, and immediately spread ¼ cup rice in pan. Top with onion slices. Pour half of spice mixture over onions, and cook 3 minutes. Add remaining rice, and add reserved spice mixture on top of rice. *Do not stir!* Cover, and cook 4 minutes.

4 Reduce heat to low, and cook 20 minutes, undisturbed. Scoop out rice from bottom, and place in serving dish with crust on top.

Per Serving: 220 cal; 4g prot; 7g total fat (1g sat. fat); 37g carb; 0mg chol; 870mg sod; 3g fiber; 1g sugars

Swiss Chard–Potato Toss

SERVES 4

VEGAN

You can use new potatoes here, but if you can find fingerlings, even better. They are long, slender potatoes with thin skins and a nutty, buttery flavor. Because they are harvested young, the natural sugars in fingerlings have not had a chance to convert to starch, so they stay firm after they're cooked but still have a creamy texture.

15 minutes 30 minutes 45 minutes

¾ pound fingerling or small new potatoes, cut into bite-sized pieces

1 tablespoon olive oil

2 cloves garlic, minced (2 teaspoons)

1 pound Swiss chard, rinsed, dried, stemmed and leaves torn into small pieces

1 tablespoon balsamic vinegar

Salt to taste

Freshly ground black pepper to taste

1 Put potatoes in large saucepan with enough salted water to cover. Bring to a boil, reduce heat to low and cook 5 to 7 minutes, or until tender. Drain.

2 Heat oil in large skillet over medium heat. Add garlic, and cook 30 seconds, stirring constantly. Add chard and potatoes. Cover, and cook 5 minutes, stirring occasionally, or until chard is wilted. Add vinegar, and season to taste with salt and pepper. Serve warm.

Per Serving: 130 cal; 4g prot; 3.5g total fat (0g sat. fat); 23g carb; 0mg chol; 190mg sod; 4g fiber; 4g sugars

Garlicky Tahini-Chard Sauce over Quinoa

SERVES 4   VEGAN

This is a delicious combination, and the lemon gives it a bright tang.

15 minutes 30 minutes 45 minutes

1 cup uncooked quinoa, rinsed

1¾ pounds Swiss chard, rinsed, dried and chopped

½ teaspoon salt, divided

⅓ cup tahini

2 tablespoons fresh lemon juice

1 to 2 cloves garlic, minced (1 to 2 teaspoons)

1 Bring 2 cups water to a boil in medium-sized saucepan. Add quinoa, reduce heat to low, cover and cook without stirring, 15 to 20 minutes, or until water is absorbed.

2 Meanwhile, in large pan, combine chard with ⅓ cup water and ¼ teaspoon salt. Cover, bring to a boil, reduce heat and cook 4 minutes, or until chard is tender.

3 Put tahini in small bowl. Stir in lemon juice, garlic and remaining ¼ teaspoon salt. Gradually stir in 2 to 3 tablespoons water to yield sauce that's creamy but not runny.

4 To serve, divide quinoa into 4 mounds on individual plates. Using tongs, arrange hot chard over quinoa, and top with tahini sauce.

Per Serving: 320 cal; 13g prot; 13g total fat (2g sat. fat); 42g carb; 0mg chol; 630mg sod; 7g fiber; 2g sugars

Cheese Beignets (page 9)

Grilled Smoked Mozzarella Sandwiches (page 18)

Cheese-Stuffed Love Apples (page 45)

Spinach and Blue Cheese Salad (page 57)

All-Day Burrito (page 25)

Red Cabbage Slaw with Baked Tofu and Peanut Dressing (page 76)

Middle Eastern Couscous Salad with Feta Cheese and Mint (page 79)

Garlicky Brussels Sprout Sauté (page 108)

7

Entrées

Easy Ratatouille

SERVES 4   VEGAN

This streamlined version of a classic Provençal dish freezes well, so double or triple the recipe for future meals. If desired, stir some chopped fresh basil into the vegetables just before serving.

15 minutes | **30 minutes** | 45 minutes

3 tablespoons garlic-flavored olive oil

2 large tomatoes, halved and sliced ½-inch thick

1 medium-sized eggplant, cut into 1-inch cubes

½ pound zucchini, sliced crosswise 1-inch thick

1 medium-sized red bell pepper, cut into 1-inch pieces

Salt to taste

Freshly ground black pepper to taste

1 Heat oil over medium-low heat in large, deep skillet. Add tomatoes, eggplant, zucchini and bell pepper. Season to taste with salt and pepper.

2 Cover and cook, stirring occasionally, until vegetables are very tender, about 20 minutes. Serve warm.

Per Serving: 160 cal; 3g prot; 11g total fat (1.5g sat. fat); 16g carb; 0mg chol; 20mg sod; 7g fiber; 9g sugars

Chickpea Dal

SERVES 4

VEGAN

You can grind the tomato, ginger and onion together and sauté the mixture with curry spices to make an authentic saucy dal. Or, to simplify preparation, use ready-made curry powder instead of the various spices. For the best results, make sure the curry powder is fresh. Serve over brown basmati rice, and garnish with cilantro and slivers of ginger.

15 minutes · 30 minutes · 45 minutes

2 cups coarsely chopped fresh tomatoes

1½ cups coarsely chopped yellow onion

One 2-inch piece fresh ginger, peeled and coarsely chopped

1½ tablespoons curry powder, or to taste

Two 15-ounce cans chickpeas, drained and rinsed

Salt to taste

1 Put tomatoes, onion and ginger in food processor, and purée until smooth.

2 Transfer mixture to large skillet, stir in curry powder and cook over medium heat, stirring occasionally, 5 minutes.

3 Reduce heat to low, and stir in chickpeas. Cook, stirring occasionally, until heated through. Season with salt to taste. Serve hot.

Per Serving: 330 cal; 14g prot; 4g total fat (0g sat. fat); 62g carb; 0mg chol; 420mg sod; 14g fiber; 8g sugars

"Salsa Verde" Yellow Squash Sauté

SERVES 6   VEGAN

Tomatillos are traditionally used to make the green salsa served with enchiladas. Here they add a light, tangy flavor that complements the sweetness of yellow squash and the earthy black beans. Look for them with the tomatoes in the produce section of your supermarket. Canned tomatillos are not a good substitute here, so if you can't find fresh, use an equal amount of green tomatoes cut into eighths.

15 minutes | **30 minutes** | 45 minutes

¼ cup chopped fresh cilantro

2 tablespoons fresh lime juice

⅛ teaspoon hot pepper sauce

2 tablespoons olive oil

1 medium-sized yellow onion, chopped

2 large cloves garlic, minced
(2 teaspoons)

1 pound yellow squash, quartered and
cut into ½-inch-thick pieces

12 ounces tomatillos, peeled, rinsed
and cut into sixths

One 15.5-ounce can black beans,
drained and rinsed

Salt to taste

Freshly ground black pepper to taste

1 Combine cilantro, lime juice and hot pepper sauce in small bowl. Set aside.

2 Heat olive oil in large skillet over medium heat. Add onion, and cook 3 to 4 minutes, or until soft and translucent. Stir in garlic, and cook 30 seconds.

3 Increase heat to medium-high. Add squash and tomatillos, and cook, stirring constantly, 5 to 6 minutes, or until vegetables are tender. Stir in black beans and salt and pepper to taste, and cook 1 to 2 minutes, or until heated through.

4 Remove pan from heat, and stir in cilantro mixture. Serve immediately.

Per Serving: 140 cal; 6g prot; 6g total fat (1g sat. fat);
21g carb; 0mg chol; 160mg sod; 7g fiber; 5g sugars

Eggplant-Tomato Sauté with Fennel and Fresh Oregano

SERVES 6 VEGAN

Instead of serving this over rice or pasta, try it wrapped in warmed pita bread with a sprinkling of feta cheese. If you can't find the slender Japanese eggplant, just substitute regular eggplant that's been peeled and cut into cubes.

2 tablespoons olive oil

1 medium-sized yellow onion, cut into 1-inch slivers

3 medium-sized Japanese eggplant (about 1 pound), halved and cut into ¾-inch slices

8 ounces Italian-style baked tofu, cubed

1 fennel bulb, thinly sliced

1 yellow bell pepper, cut into ½-inch pieces

3 tablespoons chopped fresh oregano

2 cloves garlic, minced (2 teaspoons)

6 plum tomatoes, halved and sliced

Salt to taste

Freshly ground black pepper to taste

1 Heat olive oil in large skillet over medium heat. Sauté onion 4 to 5 minutes, or until soft.

2 Increase heat to medium-high. Add eggplant, tofu, fennel, bell pepper, oregano and garlic, and cook 5 to 6 minutes, or until eggplant is tender and slightly browned. Stir in tomatoes and salt and pepper to taste. Cook 1 to 2 minutes more, or until tomatoes are heated through. Serve immediately.

Per Serving: 160 cal; 9g prot; 8g total fat (1.5g sat. fat); 15g carb; 0mg chol; 135mg sod; 6g fiber; 5g sugars

Orange-Lacquered Tofu

SERVES 4   VEGAN

This recipe proves that you don't need a lot of fancy ingredients to create a dish with sophisticated flavor. Serve with baked sweet potatoes and steamed collard greens, or cut the tofu into cubes and toss with Asian noodles.

15 minutes   **30 minutes**   45 minutes

¼ cup tamari or low-sodium soy sauce

2 tablespoons orange juice

2 teaspoons maple syrup or honey

2 teaspoons dark sesame oil

Pinch freshly ground black pepper or cayenne

Nonstick cooking spray

14 ounces extra-firm tofu, drained well and cut crosswise into eight ½-inch-thick slices

1 Combine tamari, juice, syrup and sesame oil in medium-sized bowl; whisk to blend. Season with black pepper (or cayenne, for a little more bite).

2 Spray large cast-iron or nonstick skillet with nonstick cooking spray, and heat over medium-high heat. Add tofu, and cook without disturbing, about 7 minutes, until crisp and golden. Turn over, and cook about 5 minutes, or until crisp and golden.

3 Pour in tamari mixture, and shake pan back and forth to coat tofu. Reduce heat to medium, and cook 2 to 3 minutes, or just until sauce is syrupy and tofu is glazed (sauce will get sticky if cooked longer). Serve hot or at room temperature.

Per Serving: 138 cal; 13g prot; 8.5g total fat (1.5g sat. fat); 5g carb; 0mg chol; 390mg sod; 1g fiber; 3g sugars

Ginger-Sesame Tofu with Asparagus and Shiitakes

SERVES 4   VEGAN

Tofu soaks up the flavors of sesame, tamari, ginger and garlic in this recipe, and provides a hearty complement to the mushrooms and asparagus.

15 minutes **30 minutes** 45 minutes

⅓ cup tamari or low-sodium soy sauce

3 tablespoons rice wine vinegar

1½ tablespoons dark sesame oil

1½ teaspoons light brown sugar

2 tablespoons canola oil, divided

1 pound extra-firm tofu, drained, pressed dry and cubed

1 pound thin asparagus, trimmed and cut diagonally into 1-inch pieces

1 pound fresh shiitake mushrooms, stemmed and sliced

2 cloves garlic, minced (2 teaspoons)

3 tablespoons minced peeled fresh ginger

Toasted sesame seeds, for garnish

1 Combine tamari, vinegar, sesame oil and sugar in small bowl, and stir until well blended. Set aside.

2 Heat 1 tablespoon canola oil in large wok or skillet over medium-high heat. Add tofu, and stir-fry until golden brown, about 5 minutes. Remove tofu from pan; set aside.

3 Heat remaining 1 tablespoon canola oil in same pan. Add asparagus and shiitakes, and stir-fry until tender, about 5 minutes. Add garlic and ginger, and stir-fry until fragrant, about 30 seconds. Add reserved tofu and sauce; toss well and heat through. Garnish with sesame seeds, and serve.

Per Serving: 330 cal; 19g prot; 22g total fat (3g sat. fat); 16g carb; 0mg chol; 570mg sod; 5g fiber; 4g sugars

Black-Bottom Pineapple Tofu with Cashew Coconut Rice

SERVES 4   VEGAN

Contest winner 2005 Recipe Contest Finalist Jennifer Burke, a San Franciscan Web site designer and mom of two, won this year's contest after a 12-year hiatus—her recipe for Farfalle with Carrot, Sage and Scallions won our grand prize in 1993. The secret to this recipe's success, she says, is to resist the urge to turn the tofu before it has a chance to brown.

15 minutes **30 minutes** 45 minutes

CASHEW COCONUT RICE

¾ cup uncooked basmati rice

⅓ cup raw cashew pieces

2 tablespoons unsweetened shredded dried coconut

2 teaspoons avocado or vegetable oil

1 teaspoon minced peeled fresh ginger

½ teaspoon cumin seeds

¼ teaspoon ground turmeric

¼ teaspoon salt

BLACK-BOTTOM PINEAPPLE TOFU

One 15-ounce can pineapple chunks in unsweetened pineapple juice

2 tablespoon tamari or low-sodium soy sauce

1 tablespoon balsamic vinegar

1 tablespoon avocado or vegetable oil

1 pound firm tofu, cut into 1-inch cubes

½ cup diced carrot

¼ cup diced red bell pepper

¼ cup chopped fresh cilantro, for garnish

1 teaspoon sesame seeds, for garnish

Per Serving: 424 cal; 18g prot; 18g total fat (3g sat. fat); 50g carb; 0mg chol; 517mg sod; 5g fiber; 19g sugars

1 *To make Cashew Coconut Rice:* Put all the ingredients in large saucepan. Cook over medium heat 4 minutes, or until fragrant, stirring constantly. Add 1½ cups water, and bring to a boil. Cover, reduce heat to medium-low and simmer 15 minutes, or until water is absorbed.

2 *Meanwhile, to make Black-Bottom Pineapple Tofu:* Drain pineapple chunks, and reserve liquid. Combine pineapple liquid (about 1 cup), tamari, vinegar and oil in large nonstick skillet. Add tofu cubes in single layer, and bring to a boil over high heat. Continue boiling—without turning tofu cubes—9 minutes, or until liquid becomes a thick syrup and tofu cube bottoms are dark brown. Sprinkle pineapple chunks, diced carrot and diced pepper between tofu cubes, reduce heat to medium, and cook 4 minutes, or until pineapple chunks begin to brown. Remove from heat, and toss ingredients with spatula.

3 Fluff rice with fork, and spoon onto one side of a serving dish. Transfer tofu mixture to other side of serving dish. Sprinkle with cilantro and sesame seeds and serve.

Lemony Asparagus, Capers and Crispy Tofu

SERVES 6   VEGAN

Serve this simple sauté warm, or let it cool and take it along on a picnic for an elegant entrée. In seasons when asparagus isn't abundant, substitute broccoli florets or broccoli rabe. Try a grating of regular or soy Parmesan cheese to enhance the flavors.

<table>
<tr><td>15 minutes</td><td>30 minutes</td><td>45 minutes</td></tr>
</table>

Nonstick cooking spray

8 ounces Italian-style baked tofu, cubed

2 tablespoons olive oil, divided

1 small red onion, chopped

One 4-ounce jar pimientos

3 large cloves garlic, minced (1 tablespoon)

¼ teaspoon crushed red pepper

2 pounds asparagus, trimmed and cut into 1½-inch pieces

2 tablespoons fresh lemon juice

1 tablespoon lemon zest

2 tablespoons capers, optional

Salt to taste

Freshly ground black pepper to taste

1 Spray large nonstick skillet with nonstick cooking spray. Cook tofu cubes over medium heat 5 to 7 minutes, or until brown and crispy. Remove from pan, and set aside.

2 Heat 1 tablespoon olive oil in skillet over medium heat. Sauté onion 3 to 4 minutes, or until soft. Add pimientos, garlic and crushed red pepper, and cook 30 seconds more, or until fragrant.

3 Increase heat to medium-high. Add asparagus, and cook 3 to 4 minutes, stirring constantly, or until asparagus is bright green and crisp-tender. Add lemon juice, lemon zest, capers, if using, and salt and pepper to taste. Drizzle with remaining 1 tablespoon olive oil, and top with tofu cubes. Serve immediately.

Per Serving: 130 cal; 9g prot; 8g total fat (1.5g sat. fat); 8g carb; 0mg chol; 115mg sod; 3g fiber; 3g sugars

Spicy Stir-Fry with Clementine, Asparagus and Tofu

SERVES 4   VEGAN

This robust dish is a fresh take on the classic Chinese dish that combines oranges, beef and hot peppers. It's easy to make and is terrific accompanied by steamed or stir-fried bok choy and served over steamed brown rice.

15 minutes 30 minutes **45 minutes**

SEASONING SAUCE

2 tablespoons low-sodium soy sauce, plus more for serving, optional

2 tablespoons Chinese rice wine or white wine

1 tablespoon granulated sugar

1 teaspoon dark sesame oil

2 teaspoons cornstarch

STIR-FRY MIX

1 pound extra-firm tofu, well drained

8 ounces asparagus, preferably thick stemmed, trimmed

2 tablespoons vegetable oil, preferably canola or safflower

3 large cloves garlic, minced (1 tablespoon)

1 tablespoon minced peeled fresh ginger

3 clementines, peeled and sectioned

½ teaspoon crushed red pepper, or to taste

½ clementine rind, julienned

Per Serving: 220 cal; 11g prot; 10g total fat (1g sat. fat); 20g carb; 0mg chol; 280mg sod; 3g fiber; 10g sugars

1 *To make Seasoning Sauce:* Combine soy sauce, wine, sugar and sesame oil in small bowl, and set aside. Stir together 2 tablespoons water and cornstarch in another small bowl to make slurry, and set aside.

2 *To make Stir-Fry Mix:* Cut block of tofu in half horizontally, cut each half into quarters lengthwise and cut these into cubes for total of 24. Put on paper towels, and press dry. Cut asparagus spears on diagonal into ½-inch-long pieces.

3 Heat oil in large wok or skillet over medium-high heat. Working in batches to avoid over-crowding, cook tofu on both sides 3 to 5 minutes, or until lightly golden brown and slightly crisp. Transfer to paper towels to drain.

4 Add garlic and ginger to wok, and stir-fry 30 seconds. Add asparagus, and stir-fry 2 minutes. Add soy sauce mixture; cover wok, and cook 2 minutes, or until asparagus is tender. Stir in cornstarch mixture, clementines and crushed red pepper, and cook about 1 minute.

5 Return tofu to wok, add clementine rind and stir to heat through. Serve hot over rice. Serve with additional soy sauce, if using.

Gingered Snow Peas with Tofu and Cashews

SERVES 4   VEGAN

Baked preseasoned tofu comes in many flavors. It's a quick way to add flavor and protein to stir-fries and salads. Serve this over brown jasmine rice or noodles.

²⁄₃ cup raw cashews or unsalted dry roasted cashews

Nonstick cooking spray

12 ounces preseasoned baked Asian-style tofu, cut into ½-inch cubes

12 ounces snow peas, stemmed and tough strings removed

3 tablespoons finely grated peeled fresh ginger

2 tablespoons tamari or low-sodium soy sauce

1 Preheat oven to 350°F. Spread raw cashews on baking sheet; bake until lightly toasted, 10 to 12 minutes; stir occasionally.

2 Meanwhile, spray large nonstick skillet or wok with cooking spray, and heat over medium-high heat. Add tofu, and cook, turning often, until lightly browned, about 5 minutes. Set aside.

3 Add snow peas to skillet, and stir-fry 1 minute. Add 3 tablespoons water, ginger and tamari. Stir-fry 1 to 2 minutes. Cover, reduce heat to medium and cook 1 to 2 minutes, or until peas are tender.

4 Stir in tofu and cashews, and heat through. Serve warm.

Per Serving: 350 cal; 27g prot; 19g total fat (3.5g sat. fat); 19g carb; 0mg chol; 870mg sod; 4g fiber; 5g sugars

Quinoa and Mushroom Skillet

SERVES 6   VEGAN

Quinoa might be considered a "superfood" for its superb protein content, but it's the unique nutty flavor of the tiny grain that wins cooks over. Try serving this accompanied by a salad of green and white cabbage with sliced apples tossed in a ranch-style dressing.

15 minutes | **30 minutes** | 45 minutes

2 tablespoons olive oil

1 medium-sized red onion, quartered and thinly sliced

1 cup uncooked quinoa, rinsed

2 cups vegetable stock

10 to 12 ounces cremini or baby bella mushrooms, sliced

Salt to taste

Freshly ground black pepper to taste

1 Heat oil in large skillet over medium heat. Add onion, and cook, stirring often, until golden, about 5 minutes.

2 Stir in quinoa, and cook, stirring often, 1 to 2 minutes, or until lightly toasted. Pour in stock.

3 Stir in mushrooms, cover and cook 15 minutes, or until stock is absorbed. Season with salt and pepper to taste; serve hot.

Per Serving: 180 cal; 6g prot; 6g total fat (0.5g sat. fat); 25g carb; 0mg chol; 135mg sod; 2g fiber; 2g sugars

Spinach Couscous with BBQ Tofu

SERVES 6   VEGAN

Sizzling strips of baked tofu contrast with gently flavored couscous.
Complete the meal with baked sweet potatoes.

1½ cups uncooked couscous,
   preferably whole-grain

2 tablespoons nonhydrogenated vegan
   margarine

Salt to taste

Freshly ground black pepper to taste

3 cups (5 to 6 oz.) fresh baby spinach
   leaves, rinsed

1 pound baked tofu, any variety, cubed

½ cup natural or smoke-flavored
   barbecue sauce

1 Cover couscous with 3 cups boiling water
in heatproof serving container, and let stand
10 minutes; fluff with fork. Stir in margarine
and salt and pepper to taste.

2 Put wet spinach in large, wide, dry skillet.
Cover, and steam about 1 minute, or just
until wilted. Remove, and coarsely chop. Stir
into couscous.

3 Combine tofu and barbecue sauce in skillet.
Cook over medium-high heat, stirring often,
4 to 5 minutes. Scatter tofu over couscous,
and serve.

Per Serving: 340 cal; 22g prot; 12g total fat (2g sat.
fat); 38g carb; 0mg chol; 630mg sod; 6g fiber;
7g sugars

Warm Chickpea Ragoût with Swiss Chard, Carrots and Harissa

SERVES 6   VEGAN

This dish is perfect for cool fall and winter days. Harissa is a North African condiment paste that contains chilies, cumin, garlic, coriander and olive oil. It is usually sold in a tube and can be found at most gourmet stores. It imparts a sweet heat to dishes without being too spicy.

15 minutes | **30 minutes** | 45 minutes

2 tablespoons olive oil, plus more for serving, optional

2 large carrots, peeled and cut into ¼-inch dice

1 medium-sized onion, diced

1 clove garlic, minced (1 teaspoon)

¼ cup dry white wine, such as Sauvignon Blanc

1 tablespoon harissa

¾ cup canned diced fire-roasted tomatoes

10 ounces Swiss chard, washed, dried, tough veins removed and leaves cut into thin ribbons

½ cup vegetable stock

Two 15-ounce cans chickpeas, rinsed and drained

Salt to taste

Freshly ground black pepper to taste

1 Heat oil in large skillet over medium-high heat, and add carrots, onion and garlic. Sauté for 7 to 9 minutes, or until carrots are crisp-tender. Add wine and harissa, and cook 1 minute more, or until liquid is gone. Add tomatoes, and simmer 5 minutes more.

2 Add chard and stock, and cover pan. Simmer 5 minutes, or until chard is wilted. Stir in chickpeas, and simmer 3 to 5 minutes more, or until chickpeas are warmed through. Season to taste with salt and pepper. Drizzle more olive oil on top before serving, if using.

Per Serving: 212 cal; 8g prot; 7.5g total fat (0.5g sat. fat); 29g carb; 0mg chol; 454mg sod; 7g fiber; 7g sugars

Tempeh Triangles with Piccata Sauce

SERVES 6   VEGAN

These make a great presentation!

15 minutes   **30 minutes**   45 minutes

PICCATA SAUCE

1 to 2 cloves garlic, minced
(1½ teaspoons)

2 cups dry white wine

½ cup fresh lemon juice

1 tablespoon capers, drained

½ teaspoon salt

½ teaspoon freshly ground black
pepper

1 tablespoon cornstarch dissolved in
3 tablespoons water

TEMPEH TRIANGLES

½ cup plain soymilk

1 tablespoon Dijon mustard

½ cup cornmeal

¼ cup all-purpose flour

2 tablespoons chopped fresh sage

½ teaspoon salt

¼ teaspoon freshly ground black
pepper

8 ounces tempeh

2 tablespoons olive oil

Lemon slices, for garnish

1 *To make Piccata Sauce:* Roast garlic in dry skillet over medium heat for 20 seconds. Add wine, lemon juice, capers, salt and pepper; cook about 10 minutes. Stir in cornstarch mixture; cook 3 to 5 minutes. Remove from heat, and set aside.

2 *To make Tempeh Triangles:* Whisk together soymilk and mustard in medium-sized bowl. Combine cornmeal, flour, sage, salt and pepper on wax paper.

3 Cut each tempeh piece into 3 squares, for 6 squares total. Cut each square into 2 triangles. Dip triangles in soymilk mixture, dredge in cornmeal mixture and set aside.

4 Heat 1 tablespoon oil in large skillet over medium-high heat. Cook half of the tempeh triangles about 3 minutes per side, and remove. Add remaining oil to skillet, and repeat.

5 Arrange tempeh triangles on serving plates, and top with sauce. Garnish with lemon slices.

Per Serving: 320 cal; 16g prot; 10g total fat (1.5g sat. fat); 28g carb; 0mg chol; 510mg sod; 5g fiber; 3g sugars

Tempeh with Coconut Milk and Lemongrass

SERVES 4   VEGAN

This recipe scores big on preparation ease and flavor. To extract the most flavor, pound the lemongrass's white stem end flat before mincing it. Discard the fibrous green end. Extra-firm tofu may be used instead of the tempeh, if you prefer. Serve this colorful dish over rice or noodles.

15 minutes **30 minutes** 45 minutes

½ cup light unsweetened coconut milk

½ cup plain soymilk

¼ cup creamy peanut butter

¼ cup low-sodium soy sauce

2 tablespoons minced lemongrass

2 tablespoons brown sugar

1 teaspoon crushed red pepper, optional

2 tablespoons canola oil

1 pound tempeh, diced

1 large red bell pepper, cut into thin slivers

8 ounces snow peas, trimmed

1 bunch (4 ounces) green onions, chopped

Juice of 1 lime

3 tablespoons minced fresh cilantro, for garnish

¼ cup chopped unsalted dry-roasted peanuts, for garnish

1 Put coconut milk, soymilk, peanut butter, soy sauce, lemongrass, brown sugar and crushed red pepper, if using, into food processor or blender; purée until smooth.

2 Heat oil in wok or skillet over medium-high heat. Add tempeh, bell pepper, snow peas and green onions. Stir-fry 5 minutes, or until vegetables are crisp-tender.

3 Reduce heat to medium. Add puréed mixture, and cook 5 minutes more, or until sauce thickens. Stir in lime juice. Garnish with cilantro and peanuts, and serve.

Per Serving: 520 cal; 32g prot; 30g total fat (5g sat. fat); 33g carb; 0mg chol; 500mg sod; 11g fiber; 12g sugars

Hoisin-Braised Tempeh and Chinese Vegetables

SERVES 4   VEGAN

Braising is a cooking method that begins by browning the ingredients in a little oil, then adding a bit of liquid, covering the pot tightly and cooking to blend the flavors. In this recipe, browned tempeh is joined by Chinese vegetables and a flavorful hoisin sauce, with dynamic results. This dish is delicious alone or over brown rice.

15 minutes | **30 minutes** | 45 minutes

2 teaspoons canola oil

1 pound tempeh, cut into ½-inch cubes

1 clove garlic, minced (1 teaspoon)

1 teaspoon minced peeled fresh ginger

2 large carrots, thinly sliced diagonally

1 head bok choy, trimmed and sliced crosswise into 1-inch pieces

One 8-ounce can sliced water chestnuts, drained and rinsed

4 green onions, trimmed and sliced diagonally

⅓ cup hoisin sauce

Salt to taste

Freshly ground black pepper to taste

1½ cups snow peas, trimmed and halved diagonally

1 Heat oil in large pot over medium-high heat. Add tempeh, and cook until browned, stirring frequently, about 5 minutes. Add garlic and ginger. Cook until fragrant, about 30 seconds.

2 Stir in remaining ingredients except snow peas, along with ¼ cup water. Reduce heat to low, cover and cook 15 minutes. Add snow peas, cover and cook until vegetables are cooked but still firm, about 5 minutes more.

Per Serving: 370 cal; 24g prot; 15g total fat (1.5g sat. fat); 38g carb; 0mg chol; 890mg sod; 9g fiber; 16g sugars

Pea and Red Lentil Curry

SERVES 4   VEGAN

This curry pulls in the flavors and textures of a South Indian meal. For a richer version, use regular coconut milk, and serve over basmati rice. Ripe tropical fruit such as mangoes or papayas provides a fitting conclusion.

15 minutes | **30** minutes | 45 minutes

2 tablespoons vegetable oil

3 cloves garlic, minced (1 tablespoon)

1 tablespoon minced peeled fresh ginger

2 teaspoons curry powder, or to taste

1 teaspoon ground turmeric

2 cups light coconut milk

1 cup (16 ounces) dried split red lentils, picked over and rinsed

2 cups frozen green peas

5 pieces dried mango, slivered

¼ cup raisins

3 tablespoons unsweetened shredded dried coconut

3 tablespoons mango chutney

1 Heat oil in large skillet over medium heat, and sauté garlic and ginger about 30 seconds, or until fragrant. Sprinkle with curry powder and turmeric. Add coconut milk and lentils. Reduce heat to medium-low, and cook 15 minutes more, or until lentils are softened.

2 Stir in peas, mango slivers, raisins and coconut, and cook 3 minutes more. Remove from heat, stir in chutney and serve.

Per Serving: 520 cal; 19g prot; 20g total fat (8g sat. fat); 71g carb; 0mg chol; 200mg sod; 10g fiber; 23g sugars

Vegetable-Lentil Curry

SERVES 6   VEGAN

Make this colorful main course a day ahead to give flavors a chance to meld.

2 teaspoons olive oil

1 medium-sized yellow onion, finely
   chopped (about 1½ cups)

2 tablespoons curry powder

2 medium-sized sweet potatoes (about
   1½ pounds), peeled and cut into
   1-inch chunks

1 head cauliflower (about 2½ pounds),
   stemmed and separated into
   florets

1 cup (16 ounces) brown lentils, picked
   over and rinsed

Two 14.5-ounce cans low-sodium diced
   tomatoes, with juice

Salt to taste

Freshly ground black pepper to taste

1 Heat oil in large saucepan or Dutch oven over medium heat. Add onion, and cook 5 minutes, or until softened, stirring often.

2 Stir in curry powder, and cook 1 minute, stirring constantly. Add sweet potatoes, cauliflower, lentils, tomatoes with juice and 1½ cups water. Season to taste with salt.

3 Bring mixture to a boil. Reduce heat, cover and simmer 30 minutes, or until lentils and sweet potatoes are tender. Season to taste with salt and pepper.

4 Spoon mixture into shallow bowls, and serve.

Per Serving: 250 cal; 13g prort; 2.5g total fat
(0.5g sat. fat); 47g carb; 0mg chol; 243mg sod;
15g fiber; 10g sugars

Cauliflower and Potato Curry

SERVES 6   VEGAN

This Indian-style favorite is fragrant with curry, fresh ginger and garlic.
All you need on the side is a basket of warmed naan bread, or another
flatbread, such as whole wheat pita.

30 minutes

2 teaspoons olive oil

1¼ cups thinly sliced yellow onion

2 teaspoons minced peeled fresh
  ginger

1 tablespoon mild curry powder

2 cloves garlic, minced (2 teaspoons)

4 cups cauliflower florets

4 medium-sized round white or red
  potatoes (1½ pounds), peeled and
  cut into 1½-inch pieces

1 cup canned crushed tomatoes
  in thick purée

½ cup chopped fresh cilantro

Pinch salt

1 cup frozen petite peas

1 Heat oil in Dutch oven over medium-high
heat. Add onion and ginger; cover, and cook
3 minutes. Reduce heat to medium.

2 Add curry powder and garlic, and cook
30 seconds, or until fragrant, stirring constantly.
Add cauliflower and potatoes, and cook, stirring
often, 5 minutes, or until softened.

3 Add tomatoes, ¼ cup cilantro, ½ cup water
and salt. Simmer, reduce heat and cook, covered,
15 minutes, or until vegetables are tender. Stir
in peas and remaining ¼ cup cilantro; cook,
covered, 2 minutes, or until peas are tender.
Serve hot.

Per Serving: 176 cal; 6g prot; 2g total fat (0.5g sat.
fat); 37g carb; 0mg chol; 224mg sod; 6g fiber;
6g sugars

Eggplant and Potato Curry with Spinach and Cilantro

SERVES 4   VEGAN

This curry starts out a brilliant green immediately after it finishes cooking, but its color fades to a green-brown a few hours later. Don't let the color deter you—the flavors actually improve after a day. Add steamed jasmine rice on the side to round out the meal.

15 minutes | 30 minutes | **45 minutes**

CURRY

2 tablespoons canola oil

1 medium-sized yellow onion, diced

2 medium-sized Japanese eggplant, cut into 1/2-inch dice

8 ounces Yukon gold potatoes, cut into 1/2-inch dice

1 clove garlic, minced (1 teaspoon)

1 1/2 teaspoons green curry paste

14 ounces light coconut milk

14 ounces vegetable stock

1 teaspoon light brown sugar

4 cups (7 ounces) fresh spinach, rinsed and dried

1/2 cup fresh cilantro

2 tablespoons coarsely chopped peeled fresh ginger

Salt to taste

Freshly ground black pepper to taste

SLAW

2 cups shredded cabbage

2 Roma tomatoes, sliced in half, seeded and thinly sliced

1/4 cup thinly sliced red onion

1/4 cup seasoned rice vinegar

Salt to taste

Freshly ground black pepper to taste

Per Serving: 295 cal; 5g prot; 16g total fat (6g sat. fat); 35g carb; 0mg chol; 595mg sod; 8g fiber; 11g sugars

1 *To make Curry:* Heat oil in large Dutch oven over medium-high heat. Add onion, and cook 5 minutes. Stir in eggplant, and cook 5 minutes more. Add potatoes, and cook 5 minutes more. Stir in garlic and curry paste, and cook 1 minute. Add coconut milk, stock and sugar. Bring to a simmer, then reduce heat to medium-low. Simmer partially covered, 15 to 20 minutes, stirring occasionally, or until eggplant and potatoes are tender.

2 While curry is simmering, put spinach, cilantro, ginger and 2 tablespoons water in food processor. Process until fine green paste forms.

3 Stir spinach paste into curry, and cook 3 minutes more. Season to taste with salt and pepper.

4 *To make Slaw:* Combine all the ingredients in large bowl.

5 To serve, spoon portion of slaw on top of serving of curry.

Cuban-Style Black Beans with Rice and Plantains

SERVES 4   VEGAN

Inspired by the Cuban national dish *moros y cristianos* (Moors and Christians), this robust meal is complete on its own. Depending on your mood, serve cold beer or strong, hot, Cuban-style coffee.

15 minutes **30 minutes** 45 minutes

1 cup uncooked instant brown rice

2 tablespoons vegetable oil, divided

2 firm, ripe plantains, peeled and cubed

1 large yellow onion, diced

1 green bell pepper, diced

1 vegetable bouillon cube dissolved in 1 cup water

Two 15.5-ounce cans black beans, drained and rinsed

1 teaspoon ground cumin

Salt to taste

Freshly ground black pepper to taste

½ large red onion, chopped, for garnish

½ cup chopped cilantro leaves, for garnish

1 bunch (4 ounces) green onions, thinly sliced, for garnish

1 Cook rice according to package directions, and set aside.

2 Meanwhile, heat 1 tablespoon oil in large nonstick skillet over medium heat, and cook cubed plantains 4 to 5 minutes, until just golden. Set aside.

3 Add remaining 1 tablespoon oil to skillet over medium heat, and sauté yellow onion and bell pepper 7 to 10 minutes, or until onion turns golden. Add bouillon, beans, cumin and salt and pepper to taste, and cook 5 minutes more, or until beans are heated through.

4 Spoon rice into large serving bowl or individual soup bowls, top with plantains and bean mixture, and garnish with red onion, cilantro and green onions. Serve immediately.

Per Serving: 330 cal; 12g prot; 6g total fat (0.5g sat. fat); 62g carb; 0mg chol; 610mg sod; 13g fiber; 12g sugars

Eggplant and Portobello Schnitzel

SERVES 8

Oh, what a difference lemon and capers make on oven-fried vegetables! This twist on classic *Wiener Schnitzel* is simple to prepare, yet the elegant flavors and presentation make it ideal for entertaining.

15 minutes | 30 minutes | **45 minutes**

SCHNITZEL

Nonstick cooking spray

1 cup skim milk

1 large egg

2 cups Italian-seasoned dry breadcrumbs

8 large portobello mushrooms, stemmed

2 medium-sized eggplant, sliced into ½-inch rounds

LEMON-CAPER SAUCE

3 tablespoons unsalted butter

3 tablespoons olive oil

3 teaspoons capers, drained

3 tablespoons fresh lemon juice

2 tablespoons fresh parsley, chopped

Lemon slices, for garnish, optional

Parsley sprigs, for garnish, optional

1 Preheat oven to 350°F. Coat baking sheet with nonstick cooking spray.

2 *To make Schnitzel:* Whisk together milk and egg in wide bowl. Spread breadcrumbs on large plate. Dip mushrooms and eggplant slices into milk mixture, then coat slices with breadcrumbs. Shake off excess crumbs, and set on prepared baking sheet. Spray vegetables with cooking spray, and bake 10 minutes. Turn vegetables, spray with cooking spray, and bake 10 to 15 minutes more, or until vegetables are tender and breadcrumbs are dark golden brown. Set aside.

3 *To make Lemon-Caper Sauce:* Melt butter in small saucepan over medium-high heat. Cook 2 to 3 minutes, or until butter begins to brown. Stir in oil and capers, and cook 1 minute more. Remove from heat, and add lemon juice and parsley.

4 *To serve:* Stack 1 mushroom and several eggplant rounds on each plate; drizzle with Lemon-Caper Sauce, and garnish with lemon slices and parsley sprigs, if using. Serve immediately.

Per Serving: 292 cal; 11g prot; 12.5g total fat (3.5g sat. fat); 38g carb; 39mg chol; 499mg sod; 7g fiber; 10g sugars

Late-Summer Crustless Pepper Tart

SERVES 4

Mini vegetables add visual interest to any meal, and petite sweet peppers hold a particular charm. If you can't find them, just substitute full-sized peppers cut into strips.

15 minutes | **30** minutes | 45 minutes

2 tablespoons vegetable oil

8 ounces mini sweet red and yellow peppers, cored, seeded and sliced into rings

1 medium-sized zucchini, chopped

3 cloves garlic, minced (1 tablespoon)

4 large eggs

¼ cup skim milk

½ cup shredded cheddar cheese

3 tablespoons grated Parmesan cheese

¾ cup chopped fresh cilantro, for garnish

1 Preheat oven to 450°F.

2 Heat oil in deep, 10-inch ovenproof skillet over medium heat. Add peppers, zucchini and garlic, and sauté 10 minutes, or until vegetables begin to soften.

3 Whisk together eggs, milk and ¼ cup water in small bowl. Stir in cheddar and Parmesan cheeses. Add egg mixture to vegetables in skillet. Cook 5 to 7 minutes, or until almost set, lifting the edges of the tart to let uncooked eggs run underneath.

4 Transfer skillet to oven. Bake 5 minutes, or until top of tart is golden brown. Sprinkle with cilantro, and slice into wedges. Serve warm or at room temperature.

Per Serving: 241 cal; 13g prot; 18g total fat (5.5g sat. fat); 8g carb; 230mg chol; 240mg sod; 2g fiber; 2g sugars

Mushroom Fried Rice

SERVES 4   VEGAN

This recipe is a great use for leftover rice, which keeps up to 1 week in the refrigerator. Serve this dish with a salad; fresh pineapple topped with coconut shavings ends the meal nicely.

15 minutes | 30 minutes | **45 minutes**

1 cup uncooked brown rice, or 3 cups cooked brown rice

4 teaspoons vegetable oil, divided

12 ounces cremini mushrooms, thinly sliced

8 ounces fresh shiitake mushrooms, stems and gills removed, caps thinly sliced

6 green onions, including green tops, thinly sliced

1 tablespoon minced peeled fresh ginger

¼ teaspoon crushed red pepper

3 tablespoons low-sodium soy sauce

3 tablespoons mushroom or low-sodium vegetable stock

½ cup frozen peas, thawed

1 teaspoon dark sesame oil

1 Cook rice according to package directions; set aside.

2 Meanwhile, heat 2 teaspoons oil in large nonstick skillet or wok over medium-high heat. Add half of both mushrooms, and cook, stirring often, 5 minutes, or until tender and golden. Transfer to plate. Repeat with 1 teaspoon oil and remaining mushrooms. Add mushrooms to plate; set aside.

3 Heat remaining 1 teaspoon oil in same pan over medium heat. Add green onions, ginger and crushed red pepper, and cook, stirring often, 30 seconds, or until fragrant. Increase heat to medium-high, and add rice, soy sauce and stock. Cook, stirring often, 2 minutes, then add mushrooms and peas. Cook, stirring often, 1 to 2 minutes, or until heated through. Remove pan from heat, and stir in sesame oil. Serve warm.

Per Serving: 282 cal; 8g prot; 6.5g total fat (1g sat. fat); 50g carb; 0mg chol; 461mg sod; 4g fiber; 5g sugars

Edamame Fried Rice

SERVES 4   VEGAN

Cold precooked rice is best for stir-fried rice dishes, so it's smart to make a little extra when you're boiling rice for other meals. Brown rice is used here, but basmati and jasmine rice make delicious alternatives.

15 minutes · 30 minutes · 45 minutes

1 tablespoon canola oil

2 carrots, shredded

1 yellow bell pepper, chopped

5 green onions, minced

4 cups cold cooked long-grain brown rice

3 cups cooked shelled edamame

3 to 4 tablespoons tamari or low-sodium soy sauce

1 Heat oil in large wok or skillet over medium-high heat. Add carrots, bell pepper and green onions. Stir-fry until just tender, about 2 minutes.

2 Add rice, edamame and tamari, and stir-fry until combined and heated through, about 5 minutes. Serve hot.

Per Serving: 440 cal; 19g prot; 10g total fat (0.5g sat. fat); 66g carb; 0mg chol; 840mg sod; 11g fiber; 5g sugars

Stir-Fried Wild Rice

SERVES 4   VEGAN

Now that wild rice is available precooked and vacuum-packed in many supermarkets, you no longer have to boil it for an hour to enjoy its nutty flavor.

15 minutes · **30 minutes** · 45 minutes

3 tablespoons frozen lemonade concentrate

2 tablespoons low-sodium soy sauce

1 tablespoon dark sesame oil

2 tablespoons vegetable oil, divided

2 cups sliced mushrooms

9 cloves garlic, minced (3 tablespoons)

4 ounces snow peas, trimmed

4 ounces green beans, trimmed

10.5-ounces garlic-flavored or Asian-flavored baked tofu, cubed

One 10.5-ounce package precooked wild rice

1 Whisk together lemonade concentrate, soy sauce, sesame oil and 2 tablespoons water in small bowl. Set aside.

2 Heat 1 tablespoon vegetable oil in wok over medium heat. Add mushrooms and garlic, and stir-fry 5 minutes, or until mushrooms begin to brown. Add snow peas and green beans, and cook 2 minutes more, or until just tender. Remove vegetables from wok.

3 Heat remaining 1 tablespoon vegetable oil in wok. Add tofu and rice, and stir-fry 5 minutes, or until tofu begins to brown. Stir in lemonade mixture. Fold in vegetables, and cook 2 to 3 minutes more, or until rice is coated with sauce and vegetables are heated through. Serve hot.

Per Serving: 352 cal; 18g prot; 17g total fat (2g sat. fat); 33g carb; 0mg chol; 673mg sod; 6g fiber; 9g sugars

Risotto with Asparagus and Peas

SERVES 8

Once you've discovered how easy it is to cook risotto in a pressure cooker—which traditionally requires constant stirring for half an hour or more—you'll want to make it all the time.

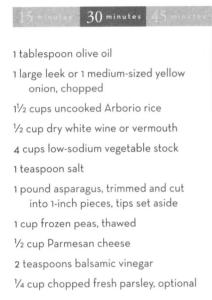

15 minutes | **30 minutes** | 45 minutes

1 tablespoon olive oil

1 large leek or 1 medium-sized yellow onion, chopped

1½ cups uncooked Arborio rice

½ cup dry white wine or vermouth

4 cups low-sodium vegetable stock

1 teaspoon salt

1 pound asparagus, trimmed and cut into 1-inch pieces, tips set aside

1 cup frozen peas, thawed

½ cup Parmesan cheese

2 teaspoons balsamic vinegar

¼ cup chopped fresh parsley, optional

1 Heat oil in pressure cooker over medium heat. Add leek, and sauté 3 minutes. Stir in rice. Add wine, and cook 1 minute over high heat, or until wine evaporates, stirring constantly. Stir in stock and salt.

2 Lock lid in place. Bring cooker to high pressure over high heat. Reduce heat, and cook 4 minutes at high pressure. Remove from heat, and place cooker in sink under cold running water 2 to 3 minutes to reduce pressure. Carefully remove lid, tilting cooker away from you to let steam escape.

3 Return pressure cooker to stove. Add asparagus stem pieces, and continue to cook risotto over medium-high heat, 3 minutes, stirring constantly. Fold in asparagus tips and peas, and cook 1 minute more, or until risotto is creamy. Stir in Parmesan and vinegar.

4 Ladle risotto into large shallow bowls; garnish with parsley, if using. Serve immediately.

Per Serving: 240 cal; 8g prot; 4g total fat (1g sat. fat); 41g carb; 4mg chol; 768mg sod; 2g fiber; 4g sugars

Two-Broccoli Stir-Fry on Soba Noodles

SERVES 4   VEGAN

Broccolini stems are tender and delicious. This cross between regular broccoli and Chinese kale adds interesting texture and peppery flavor to stir-fries.

15 minutes **30 minutes** 45 minutes

2 cups broccoli florets

One 10-ounce bunch broccolini, cut into 4-inch lengths

One 8-ounce package dried soba noodles

½ cup fresh orange juice

¼ cup low-sodium soy sauce

1 tablespoon cornstarch stirred into ¼ cup water

1 tablespoon granulated sugar, or to taste

¼ teaspoon orange zest

2 tablespoons vegetable oil

1 cup cubed extra-firm tofu

3 cloves garlic, minced (1 tablespoon)

1 tablespoon minced peeled fresh ginger

1 tablespoon dark sesame oil

1 Add broccoli and broccolini to large pot of boiling water, and blanch 2 minutes. Remove vegetables from water using slotted spoon; set aside. Add noodles to boiling water, and cook according to package directions. Drain, rinse under cold water and set aside.

2 Stir together orange juice, soy sauce, cornstarch mixture, sugar and zest in small bowl. Set aside.

3 Heat vegetable oil in large nonstick skillet over medium-high heat. Stir-fry tofu 2 minutes, or until golden. Set aside. Add garlic and ginger to skillet; stir-fry 30 seconds. Add broccoli and broccolini; stir-fry 1 to 2 minutes, or until just tender. Stir in soy sauce mixture and tofu; stir-fry 1 minute, or until mixture begins to thicken. Remove from heat.

4 Arrange noodles on platter; top with broccoli mixture, drizzle with sesame oil and serve.

Per Serving: 448 cal; 19g prot; 16g total fat (2g sat. fat); 58g carb; 0mg chol; 645mg sod; 5g fiber; 11g sugars

Thai-Style Tofu and Noodles

SERVES 6 — VEGAN

This flavor-charged dish may be served as a hot entrée or as a chilled main-course salad. A dessert of fruit and meringues will complement the Thai seasonings.

15 minutes **30 minutes** 45 minutes

3 tablespoons fresh lime juice

3 tablespoons granulated sugar, or to taste

2 tablespoons low-sodium soy sauce

3 cloves garlic, minced (1 tablespoon)

½ teaspoon crushed red pepper, or to taste

4 ounces dried soba noodles

1 tablespoon vegetable oil

1 red bell pepper, thinly sliced lengthwise

10.5-ounces Thai-seasoned baked tofu, cubed

½ cup chopped fresh cilantro

¼ cup fresh mint leaves

1 green onion, thinly sliced

½ cup unseasoned soy nuts, for garnish

1 Combine lime juice, sugar, soy sauce, garlic and crushed red pepper in bowl. Mix well, and set aside.

2 Bring large pot of water to a boil, and cook soba noodles according to package directions. Drain, and rinse well.

3 Meanwhile, heat oil in large skillet over medium heat. Add bell pepper slices, and stir-fry 5 minutes. Add tofu cubes, and stir-fry about 5 minutes, or until pepper slices soften and tofu begins to brown.

4 Combine noodles, tofu and red pepper in large bowl. Add cilantro, mint and green onion, and toss. Add lime juice mixture, and toss. Sprinkle with soy nuts, and serve.

Per Serving: 270 cal; 19g prot; 9g total fat (1.5g sat. fat); 29g carb; 0mg chol; 390mg sod; 3g fiber; 7g sugars

Singapore-Style Rice Noodles with Snow Peas, Peppers, Cabbage and Tofu

SERVES 5

This is a mild, curry-flavored dish chock-full of vegetables and tofu. These noodles are equally tasty served warm or cold. Feel free to add more chili-garlic paste, if desired.

15 minutes **30 minutes** 45 minutes

RICE NOODLES

6 ounces rice sticks or rice vermicelli

1 tablespoon canola oil

3 green onions, finely chopped

2 cloves garlic, minced (2 teaspoons)

1 teaspoon finely chopped peeled fresh ginger

2 cups thinly sliced cabbage

1½ cups thinly sliced red bell pepper

1½ cups snow peas, cut into ½-inch slices

7 ounces teriyaki-flavored baked tofu, cut into ½-inch strips

SAUCE

⅓ cup vegetable stock

3 tablespoons low-sodium soy sauce

2 tablespoons honey

1 tablespoon balsamic vinegar

2½ teaspoons curry powder

1 teaspoon chili-garlic paste

Salt to taste

Freshly ground black pepper to taste

1 *To make Rice Noodles:* Soak noodles in warm water for 20 minutes. Drain.

2 *Meanwhile, to make Sauce:* Combine all the ingredients in small bowl, and stir to combine. Set aside.

3 *To continue making Rice Noodles:* Heat oil in large nonstick skillet over medium-high heat. Add green onions, garlic and ginger, and sauté 1 minute. Add cabbage, and cook 2 minutes. Add bell pepper, sauté 1 minute, then stir in snow peas, and cook an additional 1 minute.

4 Add drained noodles, tofu and sauce, and stir to combine. Continue cooking and tossing noodles 5 to 7 minutes, or until noodles have absorbed all liquid. Serve warm.

Per Serving: 323 cal; 15g prot; 7.5g total fat (1g sat. fat); 49g carb; 0mg chol; 541mg sod; 5g fiber; 13g sugars

Garlicky Tofu with Spinach over Pasta

SERVES 4 VEGAN

A nonstick skillet is a must for this recipe—it makes the garlic cling to the tofu and form a light crust.

15 minutes **30 minutes** 45 minutes

10 ounces dried whole wheat linguine

1½ cups prepared pasta sauce

Nonstick cooking spray

12 ounces baked tofu, cut into ½-inch cubes

6 cloves garlic, minced (2 tablespoons)

6 cups (10 ounces) fresh baby spinach leaves, rinsed and dried

1 Bring large pot of water to a boil. Add linguine, and cook according to package directions; drain and set aside.

2 Meanwhile, warm pasta sauce in pot over medium-low heat.

3 Coat nonstick skillet with cooking spray, and place over medium heat. Add tofu, and cook 5 minutes, or until crisp and browned, turning often. Stir in garlic, and cook 1 minute more, or until tofu is coated with browned garlic. Transfer to plate, and cover to keep warm.

4 Add spinach to same skillet. (Add spinach in batches, if necessary, stirring to wilt so remainder will fit.) Cover, and cook 2 minutes, or until tender.

5 Divide cooked pasta among 4 individual plates. Top each with equal amounts of spinach and garlic tofu. Spoon sauce on top, and serve.

Per Serving: 506 cal; 28g prot; 15g total fat (3g sat. fat); 70g carb; 0mg chol; 847mg sod; 18g fiber; 8g sugars

Pasta with Garlicky White Beans and Swiss Chard

SERVES 4   VEGAN

Comforting and satisfying, this recipe is a hit. Serve it in wide, shallow
soup bowls so your guests get all the delicious cooking broth. If you prefer
a dish that is less soupy, drain more of the liquid off the beans. A pair
of kitchen shears makes cutting the chard quick and easy. You can also
substitute fresh spinach for the chard.

15 minutes · 30 minutes · 45 minutes

10 ounces dried whole wheat pasta
(any shape)

One 7-ounce jar sliced, olive oil–
marinated sun-dried tomatoes,
drained and chopped, with
2 tablespoons oil reserved

3 cloves garlic, minced (1 tablespoon)

1½ pounds Swiss chard, rinsed, dried,
tough stems removed and leaves
chopped

Two 15-ounce cans white beans

Freshly ground black pepper to taste

1 Bring large pot of water to a boil. Add pasta,
and cook according to package directions.

2 Meanwhile, heat oil from sun-dried tomatoes
in large skillet over medium-high heat. Add
garlic; cook, stirring, 1 minute.

3 Add sun-dried tomatoes and Swiss chard; mix
well. Cover, and cook, stirring occasionally,
3 minutes. Add 1 can beans with liquid. Drain
remaining can of beans; rinse beans, and add to
pan. Cook, stirring occasionally, until heated
through. Season to taste with pepper.

4 Drain pasta, and transfer to serving dishes.
Top with bean mixture, and serve.

Per Serving: 591 cal; 27g prot; 9g total fat (1g sat.
fat); 104g carb; 0mg chol; 239mg sod; 19g fiber;
0g sugars

Stir-Fried Pasta and Broccoli Rabe with Miso Pesto

SERVES 8   VEGAN

Miso and tahini add an interesting dimension to this nontraditional "fusion" pesto. The pairing of broccoli rabe and orecchiette pasta—orecchiette means "little ear" and aptly describes this small, round pasta—is popular in Italy's Puglia region, but any small pasta can be used. If you can't find broccoli rabe, substitute small broccoli florets, Swiss chard or spinach.

15 minutes 30 minutes 45 minutes

1 pound dried orecchiette

¼ cup pine nuts

3 cloves garlic

¼ teaspoon salt, or more to taste

4 cups fresh basil leaves

3 tablespoons white miso

4 tablespoons olive oil, divided

1 pound broccoli rabe, chopped and blanched

Salt to taste

Freshly ground black pepper to taste

1 Bring large pot of water to a boil. Add pasta, and cook according to package directions. Drain, reserving about ½ cup cooking water, and rinse. Set aside.

2 Put pine nuts, garlic and salt in food processor, and chop. Add basil, and process until minced. Add miso, and process until combined. With machine running, slowly stream in 3 tablespoons olive oil, and process until smooth and creamy. Set aside.

3 Heat remaining 1 tablespoon oil in large wok or skillet over medium-high heat. Add broccoli rabe, and season with salt and pepper. Stir-fry until tender, about 5 minutes. Reduce heat to low.

4 Add pasta, pesto and reserved pasta cooking water to wok. Stir-fry until well combined and heated through. Serve hot.

Per Serving: 330 cal; 12g prot; 10g total fat (1g sat. fat); 49g carb; 0mg chol; 295mg sod; 4g fiber; 5g sugars

Pasta with Creamy Spinach and Roasted Red Pepper Sauce

SERVES 4   VEGAN

The striking red-orange hue of this richly flavored sauce contrasts beautifully with the dark green spinach.

15 minutes   30 minutes   45 minutes

- 10 ounces dried whole-wheat pasta (any shape)
- 12 cups (two 10-ounce packages) fresh baby spinach leaves, rinsed and dried
- 1½ pounds firm silken tofu
- One 12-ounce jar roasted red peppers with garlic
- ¾ teaspoon salt
- 2 heaping tablespoons small capers, drained

1 Bring large pot of water to a boil. Add pasta, and cook according to package directions.

2 Meanwhile, put spinach in large, deep skillet or saucepan (cook in batches if necessary) with 2 tablespoons water. Stir over medium-high heat until wilted. Cover, reduce heat to low and cook 1 to 2 minutes more, or until tender. Remove pan from heat.

3 Combine tofu, peppers and salt in food processor or blender; process until smooth and creamy.

4 Drain spinach, gently pressing out any excess liquid. Combine tofu mixture and spinach in pan, stirring to blend. Cook over low heat, stirring often to heat through; do not let boil.

5 Drain pasta, and place on serving plates. Top with spinach mixture, and sprinkle with capers. Serve immediately.

Per Serving: 370 cal; 26g prot; 3g total fat (0.5g sat. fat); 65g carb; 0mg chol; 1,130mg sod; 13g fiber; 6g sugars

Vegetable Linguine with "Bolognese" Sauce

SERVES 4   VEGAN

With this dish, you can entertain elegantly and still diet. Both parts can be made ahead and combined later.

15 minutes | 30 minutes | 45 minutes

SAUCE

1 medium-sized carrot, cut in 1-inch pieces

1 celery stalk, cut in 1-inch pieces

1 small yellow onion, cut in 8 pieces

6 ounces tempeh, chopped into crumbles

2 teaspoons extra virgin olive oil

Salt to taste

1/3 cup dry white wine

1/3 cup plain soymilk

2 cups canned diced tomatoes

4 teaspoons tomato paste

Pinch freshly ground nutmeg

Freshly ground black pepper to taste

VEGETABLE LINGUINE

16 thick asparagus spears, tips and tough bottoms removed

4 large zucchini

2 large yellow squash

1 teaspoon extra virgin olive oil

1/3 cup fresh basil leaves, roughly torn, for garnish, optional

1 *To make Sauce:* Put carrot, celery and onion in food processor, and pulse until finely chopped.

2 Heat oil in large, heavy saucepan over medium heat. Add chopped vegetables and salt to taste. Sauté until vegetables soften, 3 to 4 minutes.

3 Stir in tempeh and wine. Bring to a boil, and simmer, stirring occasionally, until wine is almost evaporated, 3 to 4 minutes. Add soymilk; bring to a boil, and simmer, stirring occasionally, until mixture is soft, about 4 minutes.

4 Add tomatoes, tomato paste, nutmeg, and salt and pepper to taste. Bring to a boil; reduce heat, and simmer, stirring occasionally, until thick, 10 to 12 minutes.

5 *To make Vegetable Linguine:* Drag vegetable peeler down length of asparagus spear, removing ½-inch-wide strip. Turn spear, and repeat, making 8 to 10 strips. Repeat with other spears. Similarly peel ¾-inch strips off zucchini and yellow squash, working on all sides until you reach inner seeds. Halve strips lengthwise.

6 Bring 2 quarts lightly salted water to a boil, add strips and cook 2 minutes. Drain, then plunge vegetables into bowl of ice water. Drain again, and pat dry with paper towels. If making ahead,

Per Serving: 220 cal; 16g prot; 8g total fat (1g sat. fat); 28g carb; 0mg chol; 510mg sod; 11g fiber; 8g sugars

lightly coat strips with nonstick cooking spray, and refrigerate, tightly covered, up to 24 hours.

7 Heat oil in medium-sized skillet; add vegetable strips. Cook, stirring, until heated through, about 1 minute.

8 To serve, divide Vegetable Linguini and Sauce among 4 wide, shallow pasta bowls. Garnish with basil, if using.

Gnocchi with Fava Beans

SERVES 6   VEGAN

Happily, gnocchi are now widely available in vacuum-packed bags, which is all the more reason to use the small, oval Italian dumplings in place of pasta. If you can't find fava beans, just substitute red kidney beans.

15 minutes | 30 minutes | 45 minutes

2 tablespoons olive oil

3 cloves garlic, minced (1 tablespoon)

One 19-ounce can fava beans, drained and rinsed

One 13.75-ounce can water-packed artichoke hearts, rinsed, drained and halved

1 cup prepared roasted red peppers, drained and cut into strips

One 8-ounce can tomato sauce

¼ cup oil-packed sun-dried tomatoes, drained and chopped

One 1-pound package vacuum-packed gnocchi

Per Serving: 275 cal; 8g prot; 11g total fat (4g sat. fat); 38g carb; 14mg chol; 745mg sod; 8g fiber; 3g sugars

1 Heat oil in large skillet over medium heat. Sauté garlic 30 seconds, or until fragrant. Add fava beans, artichoke hearts and red peppers, and cook 5 minutes. Stir in tomato sauce and sun-dried tomatoes. Cook 2 minutes more, or until heated through.

2 Meanwhile, prepare gnocchi according to package directions. Drain. Transfer gnocchi to large serving bowl, and spoon fava bean mixture over top. Serve hot.

Primavera Pasta with Breadcrumb Topping

SERVES 6

Hand-twisted noodles called *pinci* (also known as *pici*) are a Tuscan delicacy. Luckily for time-pressed cooks, curly pasta noodles work too.

15 minutes | 30 minutes | **45 minutes**

8 ounces dried fusilli or rotini pasta

8 ounces green beans, trimmed

3 tablespoons olive oil

½ large yellow onion, chopped

4 cloves garlic, chopped

½ teaspoon crushed red pepper

3 medium-sized zucchini, trimmed and julienned

2 large red bell peppers, julienned

¼ cup finely chopped fresh basil

1 teaspoon chopped fresh oregano

Salt to taste

1 cup plain dry breadcrumbs

Freshly grated Parmesan cheese, as desired

Extra virgin olive oil, as desired

1 Bring large pot of water to a boil. Add pasta, and cook according to package directions. Drain and set aside.

2 Bring large pot of salted water to a boil; add green beans, and parboil 3 minutes. Transfer beans to colander, and rinse under cold running water to stop cooking.

3 Heat 2 tablespoons oil in very large skillet over medium heat. Add green beans, onion, garlic and crushed red pepper, and cook, covered, 3 minutes. Add zucchini, bell peppers, basil and oregano, and cook, uncovered, 5 minutes, or until vegetables are just al dente; do not overcook. Season with salt to taste.

4 Warm remaining 1 tablespoon oil in medium-sized skillet over medium heat. Add breadcrumbs, and sauté until golden, about 5 minutes.

5 Add drained pasta to vegetables, and toss to blend; sprinkle with breadcrumbs, cheese and olive oil, and serve.

Per Serving: 423 cal; 12g prot; 19g total fat (3.5g sat. fat); 52g carb; 4mg chol; 314mg sod; 6g fiber; 7g sugars

Zucchini "Fettuccine" with Fresh Marinara

SERVES 6 VEGAN

The key to this fresh sauce is using the reddest, ripest, sweetest tomatoes.
If they're a little acidic, stir in a teaspoon or two of pure maple syrup.

15 minutes **30 minutes** 45 minutes

1½ pounds plum tomatoes, quartered

1 cup packed fresh basil leaves,
chopped, plus 6 sprigs for garnish

⅓ cup dry sun-dried tomatoes,
softened in warm water and
chopped

4 tablespoons extra-virgin olive oil

1 shallot, minced

Sea salt or kosher salt to taste

Freshly ground black pepper to taste

8 ounces mixed summer squash
(green and yellow), ends trimmed

1 orange bell pepper, halved

8 ounces soy or fresh mozzarella
cheese, diced

1 cup chopped walnuts

Grated soy Parmesan cheese for
garnish, optional

1 Put tomatoes, basil, sun-dried tomatoes,
3 tablespoons oil, shallot, dash of salt and several
grinds of pepper into food processor, and process
until sauce resembles finely textured salsa.

2 Peel squash lengthwise on 4 sides into
paper-thin slices about 1 inch wide, using sharp
vegetable peeler. Discard soft centers, or save for
another use. Stack slices, and cut into ¼-inch-
wide "fettuccine" strips. Cut bell pepper into
paper-thin strips.

3 Put "fettuccine" strips in bowl with soy
mozzarella, walnuts, remaining 1 tablespoon
oil and salt to taste; toss gently. Pour sauce
into 6 shallow bowls, and top with "fettuccine"
mixture. Grind fresh pepper over each, and top
with soy Parmesan cheese, if using, and basil
sprigs. Serve.

Per Serving: 320 cal; 16g prot; 26g total fat (2g sat.
fat); 14g carb; 0mg chol; 590mg sod; 5g fiber;
7g sugars

Quinoa, Zucchini and Corn Enchiladas

SERVES 6

Quinoa makes a surprise appearance in these enchiladas and increases the amount of protein in this dish. The filling can be made the night before; simply warm it in the microwave before filling the tortillas.

15 minutes | 30 minutes | **45** minutes

- ½ cup uncooked quinoa, rinsed
- ½ teaspoon salt
- 2 tablespoons canola oil
- 1 small yellow onion, diced
- 1 jalapeño chile, seeded and finely chopped
- 2 medium-sized zucchini, cut into ½-inch dice
- 1 cup frozen corn kernels, thawed
- Salt to taste
- Freshly ground black pepper to taste
- 3½ cups enchilada sauce
- 8 flour tortillas
- 1 cup shredded Mexican mixed cheese or Monterey Jack cheese

1 Preheat oven to 375°F.

2 Put quinoa in small saucepan with salt and 1 cup water. Bring to a simmer; reduce heat, and cover. Cook quinoa 10 to 15 minutes, or until liquid is absorbed. Set aside.

3 Heat oil in large skillet over medium heat. Add onion and jalapeño, and sauté 5 to 7 minutes. Add zucchini, and sauté 5 to 7 minutes more. Stir in corn, and cook 1 minute more. Season to taste with salt and pepper. Stir quinoa into zucchini mixture.

4 Spray 13 × 9-inch baking dish with cooking spray. Spread ½ cup of sauce on bottom. Lay tortilla on counter, and place ¼ cup filling on tortilla. Roll tortilla up into cylinder over filling and place in dish, seam side down. Repeat with remaining tortillas and filling.

5 Pour remaining sauce over tortillas, and cover pan with aluminum foil. Bake 10 minutes. Remove foil, sprinkle cheese over enchiladas and bake 5 to 7 minutes more. Serve hot.

Per Serving: 401 cal; 13g prot; 18.5g total fat (4.5g sat. fat); 50g carb; 17mg chol; 955mg sod; 6g fiber; 8g sugars

Tortellini with Watercress, White Beans and Pine Nuts

SERVES 6

Peppery watercress and creamy cannellini beans team up for a light and luscious one-dish meal. If watercress is unavailable, 8 cups of fresh arugula or spinach may be substituted.

15 minutes | **30 minutes** | 45 minutes

Two 9-ounce packages fresh cheese tortellini

2 tablespoons finely chopped oil-packed sun-dried tomatoes plus 3 tablespoons of the oil, divided

4 shallots, minced

4 cloves garlic, minced (4 teaspoons)

½ teaspoon crushed red pepper, or more to taste

4 bunches watercress, rinsed, dried and tough stems removed

1 cup vegetable stock or pasta water, plus more as needed

Salt to taste

Freshly ground black pepper to taste

Two 15.5-ounce cans cannellini beans, drained and rinsed

¼ cup toasted pine nuts

Grated regular or soy Parmesan cheese, optional

1 Bring large pot of water to a boil. Add tortellini, and cook according to package directions. Drain, reserving 2 cups of pasta water, if using instead of stock. Toss pasta with 1 tablespoon sun-dried tomato oil, and set aside.

2 Heat remaining 2 tablespoons oil in same pot over medium heat. Add shallots and garlic, and cook until softened, about 2 minutes. Stir in crushed red pepper.

3 Add watercress to pot along with stock, sun-dried tomatoes and salt and pepper to taste. Cook until watercress is limp but still bright green, about 2 minutes. Stir in beans, add more water if necessary and heat through for 1 minute. Add pasta, and toss gently to combine. Sprinkle with toasted pine nuts and cheese, if using, and serve.

Per Serving: 430 cal; 19g prot; 16g total fat (3g sat. fat); 57g carb; 15mg chol; 520mg sod; 12g fiber; 2g sugars

Chili and Polenta Casserole

SERVES 6

Now you can have your chili and your cornbread all in the same dish! The small amount of cocoa powder in this recipe gives the chili a slight *mole* flavor. You can prepare this dish up to Step 3 the day before; simply reheat the chili in the microwave before baking.

15 minutes | 30 minutes | **45 minutes**

Nonstick cooking spray

2 tablespoons canola oil

1 cup diced yellow onion

1 jalapeño chile, seeds removed and finely chopped

2 cloves garlic, minced (2 teaspoons)

12 ounces soy "meat" crumbles

½ teaspoon light brown sugar

½ teaspoon vegetarian Worcestershire sauce

1 tablespoon chili powder

1 teaspoon ground cumin

¼ teaspoon cayenne

¼ teaspoon ground cinnamon

¼ teaspoon dried oregano

¼ teaspoon dried thyme

¼ teaspoon cocoa powder

One 15-ounce can fire-roasted tomatoes

One 15-ounce can kidney beans, drained and rinsed

1 cup frozen corn kernels

Salt to taste

Freshly ground black pepper to taste

15 ounces precooked polenta, sliced into ½-inch rounds

¾ cup shredded sharp cheddar cheese

Per Serving: 287 cal; 19g prot; 5g total fat (0.5g sat. fat); 41g carb; 1mg chol; 834mg sod; 6g fiber; 7g sugars

1 Preheat oven to 400°F. Spray 9 × 9-inch baking dish with nonstick cooking spray, and set aside.

2 Heat oil in large pot over medium heat. Add onion and jalapeño, and cook 5 minutes. Add garlic, and cook 1 minute more. Stir in soy "meat" crumbles, sugar, Worcestershire, spices, herbs and cocoa, and cook 1 minute. Add tomatoes, beans and 1 cup water, and bring to a simmer. Cook 5 minutes, then stir in corn. Season to taste with salt and pepper.

3 Transfer chili to prepared baking dish. Top with polenta slices, and cover with aluminum foil. Bake 10 to 12 minutes, then remove foil and sprinkle cheese over polenta. Bake 5 minutes more, or until cheese is melted and bubbling. Remove from oven, and let sit 10 minutes before serving.

Smoked Tofu Farfalle Casserole

SERVES 6

Here's a new twist on Mom's beloved tuna noodle casserole. We lightened the cream sauce, added lots of veggies and replaced the tuna with smoked tofu, which adds richness and depth of flavor.

15 minutes | 30 minutes | **45 minutes**

4 teaspoons olive oil, divided

1 small yellow bell pepper, chopped

1½ cups frozen baby peas

3 cloves garlic, minced (1 tablespoon)

2½ teaspoons minced fresh thyme

8 ounces dried farfalle

1¾ cups low-fat milk

3 tablespoons all-purpose flour

¾ cup grated sharp cheddar cheese

Salt to taste

Freshly ground black pepper to taste

6 ounces smoked tofu, diced

3 tablespoons Italian-seasoned
    dry breadcrumbs

1 Preheat oven to 425°F.

2 Heat 1 teaspoon oil in 6-quart Dutch oven over medium heat. Add bell pepper, and cook, stirring often, 3 minutes. Stir in peas, garlic and thyme, and cook, stirring often, 2 minutes more. Transfer to bowl, and set aside.

3 Wipe out Dutch oven; fill with water, and bring to a boil. Add pasta, and cook about 4 minutes, or until just al dente. Drain, and transfer to clean bowl. Drizzle with 2 teaspoons olive oil, and toss to coat. Return Dutch oven to stove.

4 Heat 1½ cups milk in Dutch oven over medium heat until almost simmering. Whisk together remaining ¼ cup milk with flour in small bowl, then whisk into hot milk. Cook over medium-low heat, whisking constantly, 2 minutes, or until sauce thickens and bubbles. Remove from heat, and stir in cheese. Season to taste with salt and pepper. Add pasta, bell pepper mixture and tofu, and stir to combine.

5 Mix breadcrumbs with remaining 1 teaspoon oil in small bowl; sprinkle over casserole. Bake uncovered, 20 minutes, or until golden. Serve hot.

Per Serving: 348 cal; 16g prot; 9.5g total fat (4g sat. fat); 49g carb; 20mg chol; 537mg sod; 4g fiber; 8g sugars

Penne with Broccoli and Creamy Tomato Sauce

SERVES 4   VEGAN

The silken tofu gives this sauce a rich, creamy quality, and the olives give it some punch. For the best flavor, use a high-quality pasta sauce.

15 minutes **30 minutes** 45 minutes

10 ounces dried whole wheat penne

1 pound broccoli

1 cup reduced-fat firm silken tofu

2 cups low-sodium prepared pasta sauce

½ cup chopped black olives, preferably kalamata

Salt to taste

Freshly ground black pepper to taste

1 Bring large pot of water to a boil. Add pasta, and cook according to package directions. Drain pasta, reserving ¾ cup cooking water.

2 Meanwhile, steam broccoli until just tender, about 7 minutes.

3 Put tofu into food processor or blender, and purée until smooth. In medium saucepan, combine tofu, pasta sauce, olives and enough reserved pasta cooking water to create a creamy sauce. Cook sauce over medium heat, stirring occasionally, until heated through (do not boil). Season to taste with salt and pepper, if desired.

4 Transfer pasta to serving bowl; add broccoli, and toss to mix. Top with sauce, and serve.

Per Serving: 430 cal; 22g prot; 6g total fat (0.5g sat. fat); 78g carb; 0mg chol; 420mg sod; 16g fiber; 13g sugars

Summer Salad Rolls with Spicy Peanut Dressing

SERVES 6   VEGAN

Cut all the filling ingredients about 3½ inches long. Cut crunchy ingredients, like carrots or bell peppers, the thinnest; slice softer ones, like cucumbers, thicker.

15 minutes   **30 minutes**   45 minutes

SPICY PEANUT DRESSING

½ cup silken soft tofu

¼ cup reduced-fat peanut butter

3 tablespoons sweet white miso

1½ tablespoons tamari or low-sodium soy sauce

1 tablespoon chopped peeled fresh ginger

1 small clove garlic, chopped

1 tablespoon fresh lime juice

½ teaspoon crushed red pepper

SUMMER SALAD ROLLS

Twelve 8-inch round rice paper wrappers

12 leaves Boston lettuce, rinsed, dried and thick ribs removed

8 ounces Thai-style baked tofu, cut into 24 strips

¼ seedless English cucumber, cut into thin strips

2 carrots, cut into thin strips

1 small, firm, ripe papaya, seeded, peeled and cut into thin strips

1 red bell pepper, cut into thin strips

1 ripe Hass avocado, pitted, peeled and cut into thin strips

¾ cup chopped salted roasted peanuts

½ cup fresh cilantro leaves

½ cup fresh mint leaves

2 limes, cut into wedges, for garnish

Per Serving: 450 cal; 23g prot; 25g total fat (4g sat. fat); 37g carb; 0mg chol; 510mg sod; 8g fiber; 6g sugars

1 *To make Spicy Peanut Dressing:* Purée all the ingredients, except lime juice and crushed red pepper, in blender along with ⅓ cup water until smooth. Pour into small pitcher or bowl; stir in lime juice and crushed red pepper.

2 *To make Summer Salad Rolls:* Fill bowl with hot water; immerse wrappers, 2 at a time, until soft, about 1 minute. Stack wrappers in 2 piles with damp paper towels between the wrappers.

3 Lay lettuce leaf on lower third of rice wrapper, lining up both edges. Arrange 3 or 4 strips each of tofu, cucumber, carrot, papaya, bell pepper and avocado in center of lettuce; top with sprinkling of chopped peanuts, cilantro and mint. Starting at closest edge, lift edges of wrapper and lettuce up and over filling, then fold in sides. Roll into tight cylinder like a burrito. Place roll, seam side down, on platter, and cover with damp towel. Repeat with remaining wrappers and filling ingredients. When ready to serve, remove towel, garnish with lime wedges, cilantro sprigs and mint sprigs, and serve with Spicy Peanut Dressing.

Mashed Potatoes with Home-Style Gravy

SERVES 6   VEGAN

This recipe is so easy it can be made by people who swear they can't make gravy!

4 medium-sized red-skinned potatoes
(2½ pounds), scrubbed and cut
into 1-inch dice

Nonstick cooking spray

11 ounces meatless "burgers," cut into
small pieces

4 cups sliced white button mushrooms

⅓ cup tahini

2 tablespoons low-sodium tamari
or low-sodium soy sauce

1 Cook potatoes in boiling salted water to cover, 20 minutes, or until tender. Drain; reserve cooking liquid.

2 Coat nonstick skillet with cooking spray, and warm over medium heat. Add "burger" pieces, and cook 5 minutes, or until browned. Add mushrooms, cover and cook 3 minutes, stirring occasionally.

3 Mix tahini, tamari and 1 cup water in bowl. Add to "burger" mixture, and cook 1 minute, or until thickened.

4 Mash potatoes with ⅓ cup cooking liquid, or more as needed.

5 Mound potatoes on plates. Make well in center of each mound, and spoon in gravy. Serve immediately.

Per Serving: 482 cal; 27g prot; 13g total fat (2.5g sat. fat); 67g carb; 0mg chol; 640mg sod; 10g fiber; 2g sugars

Moroccan "Meatballs" and Couscous

SERVES 6

VEGAN

This adaptation of a traditional Moroccan dish couples the sweet flavors of pomegranate juice and apricots with assertive spices. Quick-cooking rice can stand in for the couscous.

15 minutes **30 minutes** 45 minutes

1½ cups uncooked couscous

2 tablespoons olive oil

1 large yellow onion, diced

18 ounces soy "meatballs"

3 cloves garlic, minced (1 tablespoon)

One 14.5-ounce can stewed tomatoes, with juice

1 cup halved dried apricots

½ cup pomegranate juice

3 tablespoons tomato paste

2 teaspoons ground cinnamon

½ to 1 teaspoon cayenne, or to taste

Salt to taste

Freshly ground black pepper to taste

1 Bring 2 cups water to a boil in a medium-sized saucepan, and stir in couscous. Bring back to a boil, cover and turn off heat. Let stand until water is absorbed, 5 to 10 minutes.

2 Meanwhile, heat oil in large saucepan over medium heat. Add onion, and sauté 4 to 5 minutes, or until golden and fragrant. Add "meatballs" and garlic, and cook 4 to 5 minutes more, or until "meatballs" turn golden.

3 Stir in tomatoes, apricots, pomegranate juice, tomato paste, cinnamon and cayenne. Season to taste with salt and pepper. Cook mixture 5 minutes more, stirring occasionally, until heated through.

4 Transfer couscous to large serving bowl, spoon "meatball" mixture on top, and serve.

Per Serving: 484 cal; 31g prot; 8.5g total fat (0.5g sat. fat); 74g carb; 0mg chol; 763mg sod; 11g fiber; 16g sugars

Jamaican Vegetable Patties

SERVES 6 (2 PATTIES AND ½ CUP SALSA EACH)

The sweet, earthy flavors of carrots and peas temper the kick of Jamaican jerk seasoning in these Caribbean-inspired patties. For even speedier preparation, use pre-grated carrots, available in most supermarkets. To make fresh breadcrumbs, trim and discard crusts from firm, fresh sandwich bread. Tear bread into pieces, and whirl in a food processor or blender until crumbs form. One slice makes about ½ cup crumbs. The salsa can be made ahead and kept in the refrigerator for up to 2 days.

PINEAPPLE SALSA

2 cups diced fresh pineapple
(about ½ pineapple)

½ cup diced red bell pepper

⅓ cup chopped fresh cilantro or mint

¼ cup chopped green onions

¼ cup minced, seeded jalapeño chiles

¼ cup fresh lime juice

1 teaspoon brown sugar

Pinch salt

JAMAICAN VEGETABLE PATTIES

2 to 3 tablespoons vegetable oil,
divided

1½ cups chopped yellow onion

3 tablespoons jerk seasoning

3 cloves garlic, minced (1 tablespoon)

½ teaspoon salt

4 cups grated carrots

2 cups frozen peas, thawed

1½ cups soft breadcrumbs

3 large eggs

½ cup skim milk

Per Serving: 230 cal; 9g prot; 8g total fat (1.5g sat. fat); 33g carb; 105mg chol; 840mg sod; 7g fiber; 16g sugars

1 *To make Pineapple Salsa:* Combine all the ingredients, and mix well. If making ahead, cover, and refrigerate. Serve at room temperature.

2 *To make Jamaican Vegetable Patties:* Heat 1 tablespoon oil over medium-high heat in large nonstick skillet. Add onion, and cook, stirring often, 2 to 3 minutes, until softened. Add jerk seasoning, garlic and salt; cook, stirring often, 30 to 60 seconds, until fragrant. Stir in carrots. Cover, reduce heat to medium and cook 5 minutes, or until carrots are tender. Stir in peas, and cook 1 minute more. Transfer mixture to large bowl, and fold in breadcrumbs.

3 Put eggs and milk in small bowl, and whisk together. Stir into carrot mixture. Form mixture into twelve ¾-inch-thick patties, using generous ⅓ cup mixture for each.

4 Heat 1 tablespoon oil over medium heat in large nonstick skillet. Add half the patties, and cook about 5 minutes on each side, until golden. Transfer patties to plate; keep warm. Repeat, adding more oil to pan if necessary. Serve hot with salsa.

Edamame Succotash (page 109)

Tempeh Triangles with Piccata Sauce (page 135)

Summer Salad Rolls with Spicy Peanut Dressing (page 165)

Bittersweet Chocolate Pudding (page 177)

Chocolate-Caramel Fondue (page 178)

Sunny Strawberry Milk Shake (page 188)

Pomegranate Margarita (page 193)

Nutty Snack Mix (page 198)

Black-Eyed Pea Patties with Corn and Cilantro

SERVES 6   VEGAN

These patties are a wonderful main dish and may be served with tomato salsa, guacamole or cheese sauce. You may use frozen corn in this recipe, though it is also a great use for day-old corn on the cob.

15 minutes **30** minutes 45 minutes

4 cups cooked black-eyed peas, drained

3 cups corn kernels, or 4 ears corn

2 tablespoons canola oil, divided

2 teaspoons mashed garlic

2 jalapeño chiles, seeded and minced, or ½ cup canned chopped green chiles

½ teaspoon ground cumin

1 cup minced green onions

½ cup minced fresh cilantro

1 teaspoon salt

1 Mash black-eyed peas coarsely with potato masher or electric mixer. Set aside.

2 If using frozen corn, put kernels in food processor, and purée. Set aside. For cob corn, use a sharp knife to slice halfway through corn kernels, then slice kernels off cob into bowl. Use back of knife to scrape off remaining corn.

3 Heat 1 tablespoon oil in large skillet, and add garlic, jalapeños and cumin. Sauté 2 minutes, and add corn. Reduce heat to low; cook 3 minutes, stirring constantly.

4 Mix mashed peas, corn mixture, green onions, cilantro and salt; cool. Form into 6 patties about 1 inch thick and 4 inches in diameter.

5 Heat large nonstick griddle over medium heat, and brush with remaining 1 tablespoon oil. Cook patties 5 minutes per side, or until golden, crisp and heated through. Serve hot.

Per Serving: 190 cal; 9g prot; 4.5g total fat (0g sat. fat); 32g carb; 0mg chol; 300mg sod; 8g fiber; 6g sugars

"Chicken" Chow Mein

SERVES 4   VEGAN

Hungry for a quick Chinese dish that you can whip up in just minutes? This flavor-charged entrée fits the bill. Serve it family-style, in one big dish, followed by jasmine tea and fortune cookies for a final flourish.

15 minutes **30 minutes** 45 minutes

2 tablespoons low-sodium soy sauce

2 tablespoons cornstarch

2 tablespoons Chinese rice wine

6 ounces soy "chicken" strips

1 tablespoon granulated sugar

3 tablespoons vegetable oil, divided

1 tablespoon minced ginger

1 clove garlic, minced (1 teaspoon)

½ red bell pepper, cut into strips

½ green bell pepper, cut into strips

½ onion, quartered and sections separated

One 8-ounce can sliced water chestnuts, drained

½ pound bean sprouts, rinsed

2 cups chow mein noodles

¼ pineapple, cut into small pieces, for garnish

1 tablespoon dark sesame oil, for drizzling

1 Combine 1 tablespoon soy sauce, 1 tablespoon cornstarch and 1 tablespoon wine in medium-sized bowl. Marinate "chicken" strips 5 minutes. Combine remaining 1 tablespoon soy sauce, 1 tablespoon cornstarch, 1 tablespoon wine and sugar in small bowl, and set aside.

2 Meanwhile, heat large wok or skillet over medium heat. Add 2 tablespoons vegetable oil, and, when hot, stir-fry ginger and garlic for 30 seconds. Add "chicken" strips with marinade, and stir-fry 1 minute; remove strips from pan.

3 Heat remaining 1 tablespoon vegetable oil in pan, and stir-fry bell peppers, onion, water chestnuts and bean sprouts 2 minutes, or until vegetables begin to soften. Return "chicken" strips to pan, and stir in soy sauce–sugar mixture. Cook 2 minutes more, or until sauce thickens. Remove from heat.

4 To serve, arrange chow mein noodles on serving platter, and top with "chicken" stir-fry. Garnish with pineapple pieces, and drizzle sesame oil over top. Serve hot.

Per Serving: 430 cal; 15g prot; 22g total fat (2.5g sat. fat); 47g carb; 0mg chol; 400mg sod; 9g fiber; 9g sugars

8

Desserts

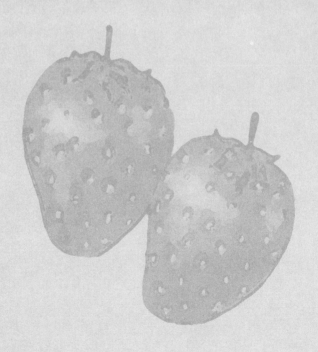

Sweet and Spicy Pecans

SERVES 6   VEGAN

Crunchy and slightly sweet, these pecans make a great dessert treat. Double the recipe, and you'll have an instant treat on hand for surprise guests.

 **45** minutes

1 tablespoon unsalted butter or peanut oil

2 tablespoons dark corn syrup

½ teaspoon salt

½ teaspoon ground cinnamon

¼ teaspoon cayenne

2½ cups pecan halves

1 Preheat oven to 250°F. Line rimmed baking sheet with aluminum foil.

2 Melt butter in large saucepan over medium heat. Stir in corn syrup, 1 tablespoon water, salt, cinnamon and cayenne. Remove from heat; add nuts, and toss to coat. Spread nuts in single layer on baking sheet.

3 Bake 15 minutes. Stir nuts, and continue baking, stirring every 15 minutes, until nuts are crisp, 35 to 40 minutes total. Transfer nuts to large platter to cool. Store nuts at room temperature in airtight container up to 7 days.

Per Serving: 230 cal; 3g prot; 23g total fat (2.5g sat. fat); 8g carb; 5mg chol; 160mg sod; 3g fiber; 5g sugars

Orange Slices with Pistachios and Cardamom

Tasting is believing when it comes to this deceptively simple dessert. Orange-flower water can be found in the specialty-foods section of supermarkets or liquor stores.

6 small navel oranges

¼ cup brown rice syrup

1 tablespoon orange-flower water
or 2 tablespoons fresh orange juice

1 teaspoon ground cardamom

3 tablespoons shelled pistachios, chopped

1 Remove peel and pith from oranges with paring knife. Slice into thin rounds, and arrange in shallow bowl.

2 Combine brown rice syrup, orange-flower water and cardamom in small saucepan. Bring to a simmer over low heat. Remove from heat, and pour syrup over oranges. Cover, and chill.

3 Spoon oranges and syrup into bowls, and sprinkle with pistachios.

Per Serving: 132 cal; 2g prot; 2g total fat (0g sat. fat); 30g carb; 0mg chol; 2mg sod; 4g fiber; 25g sugars

Summer Fruit "Cream" with Ladyfingers

SERVES 6

Elegant and creamy, this fruit dessert comes together in a snap. You can make it ahead and refrigerate it, or assemble it while the coffee brews.

12 plain ladyfingers

12.3 ounces soft silken tofu

12.3 ounces firm silken tofu

¾ cup confectioners' sugar

1 teaspoon pure vanilla extract

1 teaspoon almond extract

½ pint fresh raspberries, rinsed

½ pint fresh blackberries, rinsed

One 3-ounce package dried tart cherries

¾ cup sliced almonds, toasted, for garnish

1 Line bottom of 3-quart bowl with ladyfingers; set aside.

2 Put all tofu into food processor or blender, and purée until smooth (or beat with electric mixer until smooth). Add confectioners' sugar and extracts, and blend well. Transfer to large bowl, and gently stir in berries.

3 Pour mixture over ladyfingers, and top with dried cherries. If making ahead, refrigerate until ready to serve. Garnish with almonds just before serving.

Per Serving: 290 cal; 10g prot; 9g total fat (1g sat. fat); 42g carb; 25mg chol; 100mg sod; 5g fiber; 27g sugars

Bananas Foster

SERVES 8

This classic Southern dessert—with its flaming presentation—makes a dramatic finale for any meal.

15 minutes | 30 minutes | 45 minutes

4 firm, ripe bananas, peeled

½ cup (1 stick) unsalted butter

¼ cup brown sugar

¼ cup banana liqueur or 1 tablespoon pure vanilla extract

½ cup brandy or bourbon

1 pint vanilla ice cream

1 Cut bananas into quarters by slicing in half lengthwise and then crosswise. Set aside.

2 Melt butter in large skillet over medium heat. Stir in brown sugar. As it melts, add bananas, and turn to coat in sugar. Cook 5 to 7 minutes.

3 Add liqueur, and remove skillet from heat. Add brandy, and return to heat. When warm, flame brandy by igniting with long match; it will burn about 30 seconds. Bring to table while flaming. Serve with vanilla ice cream on the side.

Per Serving: 290 cal; 2g prot; 15g total fat (9g sat. fat); 30g carb; 45mg chol; 30mg sod; 2g fiber; 24g sugars

Mango-Ginger Pudding

A potent, delicious ginger syrup brings this dessert to life. To maximize the flavor, pound the ginger lightly to release its juices before slicing it thinly.

1 cup firmly packed brown sugar

One 3-inch piece peeled fresh ginger, pounded and thinly sliced

1 pound light silken tofu

2 ripe mangoes, peeled and diced

2 tablespoons chopped candied ginger

1 Combine sugar, ½ cup cold water and fresh sliced ginger in small saucepan, and heat over medium heat. Cook, stirring often, about 15 minutes, or until mixture turns syrupy. Cool slightly; strain syrup through strainer, and discard ginger.

2 Meanwhile, using electric mixer, whip tofu until texture is smooth and pudding-like. Stir diced mangoes and candied ginger into tofu.

3 To serve, scoop pudding into 4 individual bowls, and spoon a little ginger syrup over each serving.

Per Serving: 340 cal; 8g prot; 1.5g total fat (0g sat. fat); 78g carb; 0mg chol; 125mg sod; 2g fiber; 70g sugars

Bittersweet Chocolate Pudding

SERVES 4

Every diet needs chocolate. This creamy, calcium-rich pudding uses dark chocolate, which adds antioxidants as well as yumminess. Look for a bar that's 70 percent cacao.

15 minutes   30 minutes   **45 minutes**

2 ounces bittersweet chocolate, chopped

¼ cup low-fat milk

½ teaspoon pure vanilla extract

1 cup low-fat ricotta cheese

4 strawberries, for garnish, optional

¼ cup slivered almonds, for garnish, optional

1 Melt chocolate in double boiler over medium heat or in microwave on medium power. Stir in milk and vanilla extract until smooth.

2 Pour into blender or food processor, add ricotta cheese and purée until very smooth and creamy, about 1 minute. Pour into bowl, cover and chill at least 30 minutes. To serve, garnish with berries and nuts, if using.

Per Serving: 145 cal; 7g prot; 9g total fat (5g sat. fat); 8g carb; 15mg chol; 70mg sod; 1g fiber; 8g sugars

Chocolate-Caramel Fondue

SERVES 4

This delicious dessert fondue keeps fat and calories in check by caramelizing milk in much the same way that *dulce de leche,* the South American caramel sauce, is made. Serve it with cubes of angel food cake, toasted pound cake, strawberries, sliced bananas, pineapple chunks or vegetarian marshmallows.

¼ cup condensed milk

¾ cup fat-free evaporated milk

8 ounces bittersweet chocolate, finely chopped

1 teaspoon pure vanilla extract

¼ teaspoon salt

1 Put condensed milk in stove-proof fondue pot over medium-low heat. Cook, whisking constantly, until it turns a light caramel color, about 7 minutes.

2 Slowly whisk in evaporated milk. Bring to a simmer, whisking constantly; cook 4 minutes. Remove from heat.

3 Add chocolate, vanilla and salt, and stir until smooth.

4 Place fondue pot over tabletop warmer, and serve with dippers.

Per Serving: 49 cal; 1g prot; 3g total fat (1.5g sat. fat); 6g carb; <1mg chol; 30mg sod; 0g fiber; 5g sugars

Chocolate-Chile Mole Meringues

MAKES 36 COOKIES

These cookies taste like a cross between a dense chocolate brownie and a light, crispy meringue. Ancho chile powder is a sweet, mild flavoring now carried in the spice section of most supermarkets and gourmet shops. If you're not into spicy sweets, simply omit it.

 45 minutes

6 ounces semisweet or bittersweet chocolate, chopped

2 large egg whites

½ cup granulated sugar

2 tablespoons ancho chile powder

1 teaspoon fresh lime juice

½ teaspoon pure vanilla extract

½ teaspoon ground cinnamon

1 cup chopped pecans or walnuts

Confectioners' sugar, for dusting, optional

1 Preheat oven to 350°F. Line 2 large baking sheets with parchment paper or nonstick sheet-pan liners.

2 Melt chocolate in microwave on medium power 30 seconds. Stir, and heat 30 seconds more. Continue heating and stirring until chocolate is completely melted.

3 Beat egg whites with electric mixer on medium speed until soft peaks form. Gradually add sugar. Increase beater speed to high. Whip until stiff peaks form when beaters are raised. Add chile powder, lime juice, vanilla extract and cinnamon; beat briefly to mix.

4 Gently fold melted chocolate into egg whites with rubber spatula, leaving some streaks of white. Fold in nuts.

5 Drop batter by teaspoonfuls 1½ inches apart onto prepared baking sheets. Bake 10 minutes. Cool cookies on baking sheets, and dust with confectioners' sugar, if using. Store at room temperature in airtight container for up to 7 days.

Per Cookie: 57 cal; 1g prot; 3.5g total fat (1g sat. fat); 6g carb; 0mg chol; 3mg sod; 1g fiber; 5g sugars

Ricotta Soufflés with Mixed Berry Compote

SERVES 6

Find the freshest ricotta for this dish—it really makes a difference in the texture. The soufflés puff up more dramatically and are more tender when you use fresh ricotta. You can also serve these cold the next day.

15 minutes | **30 minutes** | 45 minutes

Nonstick cooking spray

15 ounces fresh ricotta cheese

⅓ cup plus 2 tablespoons light brown sugar, firmly packed, divided

1 teaspoon pure vanilla extract

⅛ teaspoon salt

2 large eggs, at room temperature

2 cups frozen mixed berries, thawed

1 teaspoon fresh lemon juice

1 Preheat oven to 350°F. Spray six 4-ounce ramekins with nonstick cooking spray, and wipe out excess with paper towel.

2 Whisk ricotta with ⅓ cup sugar, vanilla extract, and salt in medium-sized bowl until combined. Whisk in eggs just until combined, taking care not to overstir mixture. Spoon into ramekins, and place on baking sheet. Bake 20 to 23 minutes, or until they are puffed and set. Remove from baking sheet, and set on wire rack for 1 minute.

3 Meanwhile, combine berries, juice and remaining 2 tablespoons sugar in medium-sized bowl; and serve alongside soufflés.

Per Serving: 237 cal; 10g prot; 11g total fat (6.5g sat. fat); 24g carb; 107mg chol; 138mg sod; 1g fiber; 20g sugars

Persian "Ice Cream" Sundae

SERVES 8   VEGAN

Persians use rose water in many of their desserts. This "ice cream" exemplifies how rose water turns an everyday sweet into a festive dish.

15 minutes **30 minutes** 45 minutes

1 quart vanilla frozen soy dessert, softened

⅓ cup unsalted pistachios, crushed

1½ tablespoons rose water, or more to taste

¼ teaspoon crushed saffron threads, softened in 1 tablespoon water

½ cup vegan whipped cream, for garnish, optional

Per Serving: 160 cal; 2g prot; 9g total fat (1g sat. fat); 18g carb; 0mg chol; 65mg sod; 1g fiber; 10g sugars

Put softened soy dessert into large bowl. Stir in pistachios, rose water and saffron until well blended. Scoop mixture into freezer container, and refreeze until almost solid. Serve garnished with whipped cream, if using.

Almond Joy

SERVES 8

As delicious as a candy bar, this delicate dessert whips up in an instant. Use prepared chocolate syrup to garnish the cake.

15 minutes 30 minutes 45 minutes

One 14-ounce prepared angel food cake

12 ounces soft silken tofu

One 8-ounce package almond paste

4 tablespoons confectioners' sugar

1 tablespoon almond extract, or to taste

2 cups sliced almonds, toasted, for garnish

Chocolate syrup, for garnish

Per Serving: 470 cal; 15g prot; 23g total fat (2g sat. fat); 53g carb; 0mg chol; 380mg sod; 5g fiber; 16g sugars

1 Tear angel food cake into about 2 × 4-inch rectangles, and put about half of them into 3-quart serving dish.

2 Put tofu, almond paste, sugar and almond extract into blender or food processor, and purée until smooth. Pour half of mixture over cake pieces, and top with remaining cake pieces. Pour remaining tofu mixture over cake, and garnish with almonds and drizzles of chocolate syrup. Serve immediately, or chill up to several hours.

Tropical Papaya or Mango Squares

SERVES 6   VEGAN

This unusual dessert is delicious topped with vanilla ice cream, lime
wedges and coconut syrup. If you can't find coconut syrup, use the thick,
presweetened cream of coconut mixture used for bar drinks, which you
will find in the drink-mixes section of your supermarket.

FILLING

2 ripe papayas or mangoes, peeled,
   seeded and diced

1 semi-ripe banana, peeled and diced

¼ teaspoon ground cloves

1 teaspoon ground cinnamon

¼ cup shredded coconut

⅓ cup vegan or low-fat sour cream

Nonstick cooking spray

FILO

8 ounces filo (about 18 sheets)

Nonstick butter-flavored cooking spray
   or melted butter, for brushing

Ice cream, for serving

Lime wedges, for serving

1 *To make Filling:* Cut papayas and banana into
bite-sized pieces. Put fruit, spices, coconut and
sour cream into medium-sized bowl. Set aside.

2 Preheat oven to 375°F. Spray 8 × 8-inch
baking dish with nonstick cooking spray.

3 *To make Filo:* Remove 8 to 10 sheets filo from
package, covering remaining filo with plastic
wrap. Cut filo to fit pan. Spray every sheet or
every other sheet with cooking spray, or brush
with butter as you place them in pan. Spread
fruit mixture on top of filo layers. Remove
another 8 to 10 sheets filo from package, and
top filling with filo, spraying or brushing sheets
as before.

4 Bake about 20 minutes, or until golden
brown. Cool slightly, slice into squares and serve
with scoop of ice cream and lime wedge.

Per Serving: 170 cal; 2g prot; 3g total fat (1g sat. fat);
35g carb; 0mg chol; 125mg sod; 3g fiber; 9g sugars

Instant Lemon Tart

SERVES 6   VEGAN

Want a dairy-free lemon pie in no time? Whip this up just before dinner, and by the time you're ready for something sweet, the pie's filling will be ready.

15 minutes   30 minutes   45 minutes

12 ounces soft silken tofu

3 tablespoons confectioners' sugar

3 tablespoons frozen lemonade concentrate, or to taste

1 package instant lemon pudding mix

2 teaspoons lemon extract, or to taste

One 8-inch prepared graham cracker crust

Zest of 2 lemons, for garnish

6 lemon-flavored wafer cookies, crumbled, for garnish

1 Put tofu, confectioners' sugar, lemonade concentrate, lemon pudding mix and lemon extract in blender, and purée until smooth. For a stronger lemon taste, add up to 1 tablespoon more lemonade concentrate.

2 Pour mixture into graham cracker crust. Garnish with lemon zest and crumbled cookies, and refrigerate until ready to serve.

Per Serving: 350 cal; 4g prot; 10g total fat (2g sat. fat); 63g carb; 0mg chol; 620mg sod; <1g fiber; 18g sugars

Chocolate Banana "Truffles" with Toasted Pistachios

MAKES ABOUT 35 TRUFFLES   VEGAN

Make sure you use ripe, soft bananas for this recipe. If you freeze the truffles for a longer time, simply let them sit at room temperature for 10 to 20 minutes before serving.

15 minutes | **30** minutes | 45 minutes

6 ounces semisweet or bittersweet chocolate, finely chopped

4 small bananas, peeled and sliced into ½-inch coins

2 tablespoons finely chopped toasted pistachios

1 Put chocolate in top of double boiler over simmering water 5 to 7 minutes, or until melted. Refrain from stirring too much or chocolate will get granular. Remove from heat.

2 Add bananas to chocolate in batches, making sure banana slices are coated with chocolate. Remove banana slices with fork, and place on baking sheet lined with wax paper. Sprinkle with pistachios.

3 Place baking sheet into freezer 5 to 10 minutes, and serve.

Per Truffle: 39 cal; 1g prot; 2g total fat (1g sat. fat); 6g carb; 0mg chol; 0mg sod; 1g fiber; 4g sugars

Apple-Gingersnap Crisp

SERVES 6

This warm apple dessert is so good—and comes together so fast —you'll want to make it throughout the fall.

15 minutes | **30** minutes | 45 minutes

2 tablespoons unsalted butter or margarine

2 tart apples, unpeeled, cored and thinly sliced

½ cup apple juice

⅓ cup granulated sugar

2 tablespoons grated peeled fresh ginger

1 teaspoon ground cinnamon

2 cups dried apple slices

¼ cup candied ginger, finely chopped

20 gingersnaps, crushed, plus whole gingersnaps for garnish, optional

1 cup low-fat vanilla yogurt

1 Heat butter in large skillet over medium-high heat. Sauté fresh apple slices 5 minutes, or until tender. Stir in juice, sugar, fresh ginger and cinnamon. Cook 5 minutes, or until liquid is syrupy.

2 Add dried apple slices and candied ginger. Reduce heat to medium, and cook 3 minutes more, or until heated through.

3 Sprinkle bottom of 2-quart bowl with ½ cup crushed gingersnaps. Stir remaining crumbs into apple mixture. Layer apple mixture and yogurt in bowl. Garnish with whole gingersnaps, if using. Serve warm.

Per Serving: 342 cal; 4g prot; 7g total fat (3.5g sat. fat); 70g carb;14mg chol; 210mg sod; 5g fiber; 38g sugars

Crunchy Chocolate Truffle Pie

SERVES 12   VEGAN

Contest winner   Shannon Allison-Leszek spends her spare
time cooking delicious vegan food that even her non-veg family members
love. The surprising list of ingredients in this recipe adds up to chocolate
heaven—hats off to Shannon for finding just the right balance of flavors and
textures. (She confided that it took several tries to get it just right.) This
was the first-place winner in the 2005 *Vegetarian Times* Recipe Contest.

15 minutes | **30 minutes** | 45 minutes

1 cup semisweet chocolate chips

12 ounces firm silken tofu

½ cup pure maple syrup

1 cup creamy peanut butter

One 9-inch prepared graham cracker
   crust

½ cup chopped chocolate-covered
   pretzels

1 Put chocolate chips in microwave-safe bowl,
and microwave on high 30 seconds. Stir
chocolate, and heat 30 seconds more. Repeat
heating and stirring until chocolate is just
melted. Set aside.

2 Combine tofu and maple syrup in food
processor, and blend 3 minutes, or until smooth.
Add peanut butter, and process until smooth.
Add melted chocolate, and process once more
until smooth.

3 Pour peanut butter–chocolate mixture into
pie crust, smoothing the top; refrigerate
20 minutes. Sprinkle pretzels over top, and
serve, or refrigerate until ready to eat.

Per Serving: 332 cal; 9g prot; 20g total fat (6g sat.
fat); 34g carb; 0mg chol; 220mg sod; 3g fiber;
22g sugars

9

Beverages

Cucumber, Lime and Mint Agua Fresca

SERVES 5   VEGAN

Here's a cool, refreshing drink that never fails to pick you up on hot summer days. Serve with plenty of ice, lime wedges and mint sprigs. If desired, top with a splash of club soda.

15 minutes 30 minutes 45 minutes

1 English cucumber (about 1 pound), peeled and cut into 1-inch pieces

1 tablespoon chopped fresh mint

⅓ cup agave syrup

¼ cup fresh lime juice

Ice cubes, for serving

Mint sprigs, for garnish

Put cucumber, mint and 2 cups water in blender. Blend until smooth. Pour through strainer into pitcher, pressing down on solids to extract juice. Whisk in 2 cups water, agave syrup and lime juice. Serve over ice garnished with mint sprigs.

Per Serving: 73 cal; <1g prot; 0g total fat (0g sat. fat); 18g carb; 0mg chol; 1mg sod; 0g fiber; 17g sugars

Sunny Strawberry Milk Shake

SERVES 1

Inspired by the old-fashioned soda fountain treat, this refreshing drink is a perfect mid-morning or afternoon snack. The fruit gives it natural sweetness; the tofu increases the protein content. And adding ground flaxseeds contributes a pleasant, slightly nutty flavor—plus fiber and omega-3s.

15 minutes 30 minutes 45 minutes

½ cup frozen strawberries

1 cup low-fat (2 percent) milk

4 ounces (¼ cup) light silken tofu

1 tablespoon frozen orange juice concentrate

1 tablespoon ground flaxseeds, optional

Put all the ingredients, in order, in blender. Whirl until smooth and frothy. Pour into tall glass, and drink immediately.

Per Serving: 206 cal; 12g prot; 6g total fat (3g sat. fat); 27g carb; 18mg chol; 131mg sod; 2g fiber; 23g sugars

Creamy Wake-Up Shake

SERVES 3   VEGAN

To really speed things up, make a double or triple batch of the soymilk-juice-vanilla-syrup-ginger mixture, and refrigerate it in an airtight container. In the morning, put 2 cups of it in the blender with the fruit and ice, then just whip and sip.

15 minutes 30 minutes 45 minutes

1 cup vanilla soymilk

1 cup tropical juice blend

1 tablespoon maple syrup, honey or brown rice syrup

1 teaspoon pure vanilla extract

1 teaspoon grated peeled fresh ginger, optional

2 cups fresh or frozen sliced fruit, such as melon, peaches, strawberries or bananas

½ cup crushed ice

Whole fresh berries, for garnish, optional

1 Combine soymilk, juice, maple syrup, vanilla extract and ginger, if using, in blender, and process until smooth.

2 Add fruit and ice, and process until blended. Garnish with berries, if using. Serve immediately.

Per Serving: 217 cal; 4g prot; 2g total fat (0g sat. fat); 48g carb; 0mg chol; 44mg sod; 5g fiber; 35g sugars

Old-Fashioned Strawberry-Orange Soda

SERVES 8   VEGAN

The quality of this homemade soda depends on the ripeness of the berries. For more strawberry flavor, use another ½ cup berries for the purée and cut back the orange juice by about ½ cup. Add just enough soda for spritz. Delish!

15 minutes ~~30 minutes~~ ~~45 minutes~~

2 to 3 cups sliced strawberries, washed and hulled

½ cup cooled Simple Syrup (see recipe below)

1½ to 2 cups fresh orange juice

3 tablespoons fresh lemon juice

1 quart club soda, or to taste

Put berries in blender or food processor, and process; pour through strainer into pitcher for smooth purée. Add syrup. Stir in orange and lemon juices; add soda to taste. Serve chilled.

Simple Syrup

To sweeten fruit purées, fruit soups and even iced tea in the summer, it's great to have a simple sugar syrup on hand. Once made, it will keep almost indefinitely in a tightly closed container in the refrigerator. Combine 2 cups granulated sugar and 2 cups water in small saucepan. Heat over low heat, and stir until sugar is completely dissolved. Increase heat to medium-high, and bring to a boil. Reduce heat to low, and cook 3 to 5 minutes. Cool, and refrigerate.

Per Serving: 70 cal; 1g prot; 0g total fat (0g sat. fat); 17g carb; 0mg chol; 25mg sod; <1g fiber; 14g sugars

Homemade Ginger Ale

SERVES 16   VEGAN

You haven't tasted ginger ale until you've had a glass of this brew . . . you'll
never go back to the canned stuff again! The fresh ginger adds zip without
being too spicy. And besides being totally irresistible, it's super simple to make.

15 minutes | 30 minutes | **45** minutes

2 cups light brown sugar

8 ounces fresh ginger, peeled and cut
    into ¼-inch-thick coins

1 cinnamon stick

Pinch cayenne

Ice cubes, for serving

3 quarts sparkling water, for serving

Per Serving: 103 cal; 0g prot; 0g total fat (0g sat. fat);
27g carb; 0mg chol; 12mg sod; 0g fiber; 25g sugars

1 Bring sugar, ginger, cinnamon stick and
2 cups water to a boil in large saucepan. Simmer
5 minutes, then remove from heat, and stir in
cayenne. Let cool.

2 Strain syrup into small pitcher, and discard
ginger and cinnamon. Cover, and refrigerate
until ready to use.

3 To serve, ladle ¼ cup ginger syrup into
tumbler filled with ice. Top with ¾ cup
sparkling water, and stir.

Tropical Refresher

SERVES 6   VEGAN

Supermarkets and natural-food stores now stock an amazing array of
tropical juices and nectars. You can use our blend, or create your own
variation for a delicious cocktail to welcome your guests.

15 minutes | 30 minutes | 45 minutes

2 cups mango nectar

2 cups guava nectar or passion fruit juice

2 cups pineapple juice

Ice cubes, for serving

¾ cup rum, optional

6 lime slices, for garnish

Per Serving: 140 cal; 1g prot; 0g total fat (0g sat. fat);
37g carb; 0mg chol; 5mg sod; 1g fiber; 35g sugars

1 Combine fruit nectars and juice in large
pitcher; chill.

2 To serve, put several ice cubes in each of 6 tall
glasses. Add shot of rum to each one, if using,
and fill glasses with juice mixture. Stir to mix,
and garnish with lime slices.

Posada Punch

SERVES 8   VEGAN

¡Salud! This makes a dazzling party drink whether poured from a frosty pitcher or doubled or tripled and serve d in a punch bowl. The frozen mango chunks (found in the freezer section of most supermarkets) keep the punch cool without diluting it. The pomegranate seeds add color.

15 minutes   30 minutes   45 minutes

2 cups mango juice

1 cup tequila blanco

½ cup Triple Sec

¼ cup fresh lime juice

1 cup frozen mango chunks

2 limes, sliced

¼ cup pomegranate seeds, optional

Ice cubes

Combine mango juice, tequila, Triple Sec and lime juice in large pitcher. Add mango chunks, 1 sliced lime and pomegranate seeds, if using. Stir in about 2 cups ice cubes. Serve in glasses garnished with remaining lime slices.

Per Serving: 166 cal; <1g prot; 0.5g total fat (0g sat. fat); 19g carb; 0mg chol; 15mg sod; 2g fiber; 15g sugars

Watermelon Margaritas

SERVES 4   VEGAN

Guests will flip for these frozen watermelon margaritas that get additional sweetness and citrus flavor from Triple Sec, an orange-flavored liqueur.

15 minutes   30 minutes   45 minutes

2 cups diced, seeded watermelon, frozen

¾ cup tequila

⅓ cup Triple Sec

1 tablespoon granulated sugar, plus more as needed

2 tablespoons fresh lime juice

2 cups crushed ice

Lime slices, for garnish, optional

Orange slices, for garnish, optional

Put frozen watermelon, tequila, Triple Sec, sugar and lime juice in blender; process until smooth. Add ice; process again until smooth. Serve in glasses rimmed with sugar, and garnish with lime and orange slices, if using.

Per Serving: 220 cal; 1g prot; 0g total fat (0g sat. fat); 18g carb; 0mg chol; 0mg sod; 0g fiber; 15g sugars

Pomegranate Margarita

SERVES 1
VEGAN

If only a couple of people are likely to imbibe, you can make these to order in a cocktail shaker. Otherwise, multiply this recipe by 8 to 12, and mix everything together in a large pitcher.

15 minutes 30 minutes 45 minutes

Margarita or coarse salt, for rimming glass

¼ to ⅓ cup pomegranate juice

2 tablespoons tequila

2 tablespoons Triple Sec

2 tablespoons fresh lime juice

Ice cubes, for serving

1 Put a bit of water on one shallow plate and a bit of salt on another shallow plate. Dip edge of glass into water, then salt, to coat rim.

2 In cocktail shaker, combine pomegranate juice, tequila, Triple Sec and lime juice. Add ice cubes, and shake well. Pour over ice into glass.

Per serving: 190 cal; 0g prot; 0g total fat (0g sat. fat); 16g carb; 0mg chol; 0mg sod; 0g fiber; 13g sugars

Mexican Hot Chocolate

SERVES 8
VEGAN

In Mexico, round boxes of Abuelita or Ibarra chocolate are as familiar and well-loved as Nestlé's Nesquick and Hershey's syrup are in the United States. The individually wrapped tablets of chocolate inside are laced with canela (Mexican cinnamon) and stone-ground cocoa nibs, which give Mexican hot chocolate its distinctive flavor and earthy texture. Both brands are becoming more common in national supermarkets, but you can always find them in Mexican markets or at mexgrocer.com.

15 minutes 30 minutes 45 minutes

1 quart water or milk

One 3-ounce Mexican chocolate tablet, such as Ibarra or Abuelita, coarsely chopped

8 cinnamon sticks, for garnish

Heat 1 cup water with chocolate in large saucepan over medium heat. Stir until chocolate has melted. Add remaining water, and bring to a simmer. Remove from heat, and beat with whisk or electric mixer on low, until foamy. Serve in mugs garnished with cinnamon sticks.

Per Serving: 50 cal; 1g prot; 3g total fat (1.5g sat. fat); 6g carb; 0mg chol; 1mg sod; 1g fiber; 0g sugars

Café Brûlot

SERVES 8

VEGAN

If you prepare this at the table, it is even more festive—ladling flaming coffee into cups is a showstopper. Remove citrus zest with a paring knife or zester, avoiding any white pith.

15 minutes

8 sugar cubes

Zest of 1 orange

Zest of ½ lemon

½ cup brandy or bourbon

1 small cinnamon stick

½ teaspoon whole cloves

3 cups hot, freshly brewed dark roast coffee, preferably with chicory

1 Rub sugar cubes in orange and lemon zest. Put sugar cube in each of 8 demitasse cups or small mugs.

2 Heat brandy, cinnamon stick, orange and lemon zests and cloves together in chafing dish. Flame mixture by igniting with long match, and carefully add hot coffee. Stir, and ladle mixture into prepared cups.

Per Serving: 50 cal; 0g prot; 0g total fat (0g sat. fat); 3g carb; 0mg chol; 0mg sod; 3g fiber; 5g sugars

10

Kidz

Carrot-Raisin Waffles

SERVES 6

These waffles have it all—the good-grain richness of whole wheat, the spicy sweetness of cinnamon and the healthful fiber of carrots and raisins.

15 minutes 30 minutes **45 minutes**

Nonstick cooking spray

1½ cups whole wheat pastry flour

3 tablespoons light brown sugar

1½ teaspoons baking powder

1 teaspoon ground cinnamon

½ teaspoon baking soda

¼ teaspoon salt

2 large eggs

1 cup low-fat buttermilk

2 tablespoons vegetable oil

¾ cup finely grated carrots

½ cup raisins

1 Lightly coat waffle iron with nonstick cooking spray, and preheat. Preheat oven to 200°F.

2 Whisk together flour, sugar, baking powder, cinnamon, baking soda and salt in large bowl.

3 Whisk together eggs, buttermilk and oil in medium-sized bowl, and stir into flour mixture. Fold in carrots and raisins.

4 Ladle ½ cup batter (or amount recommended in manufacturer's directions) onto waffle iron. Close lid, and cook 4 minutes, or until golden. Gently open lid, and remove waffle with fork. Serve immediately, or transfer to baking sheet and keep warm in oven. Repeat with remaining batter, lightly coating waffle iron with cooking spray each time.

Per Serving: 219 cal; 8g prot; 7g total fat (1g sat. fat); 33g carb; 72mg chol; 339mg sod; 4g fiber; 10g sugars

Blueberry and Gingersnap Parfait with Vanilla Yogurt

SERVES 6

Your kids can assemble this pretty, super-easy dessert. Feel free to play with whatever berries or cookies you like for this recipe.

15 minutes 30 minutes 45 minutes

2¼ cups low-fat vanilla yogurt

1 pint (2 cups) blueberries

1 cup crushed gingersnap cookies

Per Serving: 236 cal; 8g prot; 3.5g total fat (1.5g sat. fat); 43g carb; 8mg chol; 214mg sod; 2g fiber; 32g sugars

Set six 8-ounce glasses or cups on the counter. Spoon 2 tablespoons yogurt into each glass followed with 2 tablespoons berries and 1 tablespoon cookie crumbs. Repeat this layering once, and end with another layer of yogurt. Let sit for 10 minutes, and serve.

Crispy Breakfast Bars

SERVES 4   VEGAN

If you're a fan of Rice Krispies™ treats, you'll love these crunchy-chewy bars. They get fiber and iron from whole-grain puffed cereal and protein from almond butter.

15 minutes 30 minutes **45 minutes**

7 cups whole-grain puffed cereal

¾ cup dried cranberries

¾ cup raisins or dried blueberries

1 teaspoon ground cinnamon

¾ cup brown rice syrup or honey

¾ cup almond butter

2 tablespoons soy margarine or unsalted butter

Per Serving: 220 cal; 4g prot; 9.5g total fat (1.5g sat. fat); 33g carb; 4mg chol; 20mg sod; 2g fiber; 23g sugars

1 Stir together cereal, dried fruit and cinnamon in large bowl.

2 Put syrup, almond butter and soy margarine in large, microwave-safe measuring cup. Microwave 1½ minutes on high, or until hot and margarine has melted. Stir well, then pour over cereal mixture. Stir to coat.

3 Dampen hands with cold water. Press cereal mixture firmly into 9 × 9-inch baking pan, re-wetting hands if necessary to keep mixture from sticking. Freeze 30 minutes. Cut into 15 bars, and store in refrigerator up to 5 days.

Nutty Snack Mix

SERVES 4   VEGAN

Dried fruit adds complex carbs and fiber to this healthful, portable and unusually good trail mix. It will keep up to 5 days in an airtight container.

15 minutes | **30** minutes | 45 minutes

½ cup whole natural almonds (skin on)

½ cup walnut pieces

⅓ cup roasted soy nuts, salted or plain

¼ cup dried blueberries, coarsely chopped

1 slice candied ginger, very finely chopped, optional

1 Preheat oven to 350°F.

2 Spread almonds and walnuts on baking sheet. Bake 6 minutes; stir, and bake 4 minutes longer. When cool enough to handle, cut almonds in half crosswise.

3 Combine roasted nuts, soy nuts, blueberries and ginger, if using, in medium-sized bowl.

Per Serving: 280 cal; 9g prot; 21g total fat (2g sat. fat); 16g carb; 0mg chol; 9mg sod; 3.5g fiber; 5g sugars

Apple-Oat Bars

SERVES 16

VEGAN

Charmingly old-fashioned, these wholesome bars pair the comforting flavors of apples and oats. They're the perfect snack to pack in a lunch box or enjoy with a glass of milk.

15 minutes · 30 minutes · **45** minutes

Nonstick cooking spray, optional

1½ cups unbleached all-purpose flour

1 cup old-fashioned rolled oats

1 cup packed light brown sugar

¾ teaspoon baking powder

½ teaspoon salt

½ teaspoon ground cinnamon

¼ teaspoon ground nutmeg

⅓ cup apple cider or apple juice

3 tablespoons vegetable oil

3 cups peeled, chopped tart apples, such as Granny Smith

¼ cup coarsely chopped walnuts, toasted, optional

1 Preheat oven to 350°F. Lightly grease 9 × 9-inch baking pan, or coat with nonstick cooking spray.

2 Mix flour, oats, brown sugar, baking powder, salt, cinnamon and nutmeg in large bowl. Using fork or fingertips, work in cider and oil until mixture resembles coarse crumbs.

3 Press about 1½ cups oat mixture firmly into bottom of prepared pan. Sprinkle with chopped apples. Mix walnuts, if using, into remaining oat mixture. Sprinkle evenly over apples, and pat into even layer.

4 Bake 30 to 35 minutes, or until top is golden and apples are tender when pierced with a fork. Cool completely on wire rack before cutting into bars.

Per serving: 150 cal; 2g prot; 3g total fat (0g sat. fat); 29g carb; 0mg chol; 100mg sod; 1g fiber; 16g sugars

No-Bake Almond-Oat Energy Bites

MAKES TWENTY-FOUR 1-INCH BALLS

Contest winner Necessity is the mother of invention for Holly Mell, third-place winner in the 2005 *Vegetarian Times* Recipe Contest. A vegetarian since she was 10, she's been cooking non-meat meals for herself for a long time and has also had to find ways around her food allergies. And what a way she's found with this recipe! If you've ever been let down by homemade granola bars that taste a little too, um, "healthy," give these yummy nuggets a try.

15 minutes **30 minutes** 45 minutes

2½ cups rolled oats, regular or quick cooking, divided

½ cup raw pumpkin seeds (*pepitas*), divided

½ cup raisins

2 tablespoons raw sunflower seeds

1 teaspoon ground cinnamon

½ cup almond butter

⅓ cup plus 1 tablespoon honey

2 tablespoons barley malt syrup

1 teaspoon pure vanilla extract

1 Grind ½ cup oats and ¼ cup pumpkin seeds in food processor until powdery. Transfer to medium-sized bowl; set aside.

2 Combine remaining 2 cups oats, remaining ¼ cup pumpkin seeds, raisins, sunflower seeds and cinnamon in large bowl. Stir in almond butter, honey, barley malt syrup and vanilla extract until soft dough forms.

3 Moisten hands, and roll dough into 1-inch balls. Coat balls in oat–pumpkin seed powder. Place in freezer 20 minutes to set, then serve or store in the refrigerator up to 5 days.

Per Ball: 148 cal; 5g prot; 6g total fat (1g sat. fat); 21g carb; 0mg chol; 2mg sod; 2g fiber; 8g sugars

Easy Tostadas

SERVES 6

For those nights when everyone has to eat at a different time, simply set out the components of this meal-in-a-wrap, and let the gang make their own. If you can't find poblano chiles, use canned green chiles instead.

15 minutes **30 minutes** 45 minutes

1 teaspoon plus 2 tablespoons vegetable oil, divided

1 poblano chile, cut into long, thin strips

One 15.5-ounce can pinto beans, drained and rinsed

One 15.5-ounce can hominy, drained and rinsed

6 ounces Mexican-flavored soy "ground meat"

1 cup prepared salsa, plus more for drizzling

1 tablespoon chili powder, or to taste

1 tablespoon fresh lime juice, or to taste

6 whole wheat tortillas

6 large lettuce leaves, rinsed and dried

½ cup shredded reduced-fat cheddar cheese

1 Heat 1 teaspoon oil in large skillet over medium heat, and sauté poblano strips 1 minute, or until golden. Transfer to small plate.

2 Heat remaining 2 tablespoons oil in skillet over medium heat, and add beans, hominy, soy "meat," salsa, chili powder and lime juice. Cook 7 minutes, or until sauce is thick.

3 Meanwhile, warm tortillas on skillet or griddle over medium heat or in microwave. Place tortillas on individual serving plates. Put 1 lettuce leaf on each tortilla, spoon filling mixture onto lettuce leaves, top with poblano strips and cheese, and serve.

Per Serving: 336 cal; 16g prot; 8g total fat (2g sat. fat); 49g carb; 7mg chol; 920mg sod; 24g fiber; 2g sugars

Mexican-Style Panini

SERVES 4

Rich in fiber and protein, these not-too-spicy bean-filled panini are a quick, tasty lunch (for adults, too) or after-school snack.

15 minutes 30 minutes 45 minutes

Four 6-inch whole wheat pita pockets

8 ounces fat-free vegetarian refried beans

1 roasted red bell pepper, cut into 4 pieces (drain and rinse pepper, if jarred)

4 tablespoons mild salsa

4 slices regular or soy cheddar cheese

1 Cut an opening across top of each pita, just large enough to place fillings inside. Spread ¼ cup refried beans inside each pita. Add 1 piece red pepper, 1 tablespoon salsa and 1 slice cheese to each pita.

2 Place large skillet over medium-low heat. Add pitas. Place another skillet over pitas, making sure it rests evenly on pitas. Cook pita panini 1 minute. Remove top skillet, flip panini, place top skillet back on panini and cook 1 more minute, or until lightly browned. Serve hot.

Per Serving: 187 cal; 10g prot; 2.5g total fat (0g sat. fat); 30g carb; 0mg chol; 998mg sod; 6g fiber; 1g sugars

Peanut Butter Panini with Apples and Raisins

SERVES 4

Raisins and apples add fiber and flavor to the beloved PB&J, and low-fat whole-grain waffles are a fun, healthful alternative to bread. Try these for breakfast.

15 minutes **30 minutes** 45 minutes

¼ cup golden raisins

¼ cup peanut butter

2 tablespoons honey

Eight 3¾-inch round, low-fat whole-grain waffles

1 Fuji apple, cored and sliced into ⅛-inch-thick pieces

4 tablespoons all-fruit jam, such as raspberry or strawberry

2 teaspoons unsalted butter

1 Combine raisins, peanut butter and honey in small bowl; stir to blend. Divide among 4 waffles, and spread to cover. Top each with several apple slices (about 5).

2 Spread 1 tablespoon jam on each of 4 remaining waffles; place jam side down on peanut butter-topped waffles.

3 Heat 1 teaspoon butter in large nonstick skillet over medium heat. Add waffle sandwiches and reduce heat to medium-low. Place another skillet over waffles, making sure it rests evenly on waffles. Cook waffle panini 1½ minutes. Flip panini; add remaining 1 teaspoon butter to skillet, and slide panini around skillet to coat with melted butter. Replace top skillet, and cook 1 minute more, or until lightly browned. Cut each panini in half, and serve hot with any remaining apple slices on the side.

Per Serving: 391 cal; 10g prot; 12.5g total fat (3.5g sat. fat); 64g carb; 10mg chol; 756mg sod; 5g fiber; 28g sugars

Nutty Noodles

Refrigerate any leftovers. To make the mixture creamy again, add a spoonful or two of boiling water, and toss.

15 minutes | 30 minutes | 45 minutes

12 ounces thin dried spaghetti or other pasta

2 tablespoons dark sesame oil, divided

½ cup smooth peanut or cashew butter

¼ cup low-sodium soy sauce

2 tablespoons rice or red wine vinegar

1 tablespoon coarsely chopped peeled fresh ginger

2 teaspoons honey

1 or 2 cloves garlic, crushed (1 to 2 teaspoons)

2 green onions or 1 rib celery, chopped

½ cucumber, peeled, seeded and diced, or ½ red bell pepper, diced

1 Cook noodles according to package directions. Drain, rinse with cold water and drain again. Transfer to medium-sized bowl. Toss with 1 tablespoon oil.

2 Put remaining 1 tablespoon oil, nut butter, soy sauce, ¼ cup water, vinegar, ginger, honey and garlic into blender. Purée 10 to 20 seconds, or until smooth and thick but pourable. If needed, thin with 1 teaspoon or so water.

3 Add dressing to noodles, and toss well, coating pasta thoroughly. Top with chopped vegetables and serve warm or at room temperature.

Per Serving: 380 cal; 13g prot; 17g total fat (3g sat. fat); 48g carb; 0mg chol; 360mg sod; 4g fiber; 6g sugars

Broccoli with Orange Sauce

SERVES 4 VEGAN

Here's a quick and easy way to add some excitement (and extra vitamin C) to cancer-fighting broccoli. The orange sauce can also be used to dress up just about any steamed vegetable, such as cauliflower, green beans or asparagus.

15 minutes 30 minutes 45 minutes

8 cups broccoli florets (about 2 large heads)

1 tablespoon soy margarine or unsalted butter

2 cloves garlic, minced (2 teaspoons)

1 teaspoon minced peeled fresh ginger

½ cup fresh orange juice

¼ teaspoon salt

⅛ teaspoon freshly ground black pepper

1 Steam broccoli, covered, 6 minutes, or until crisp-tender.

2 Meanwhile, melt margarine in small skillet over medium heat. Add garlic and ginger, and cook, stirring often, 1 minute. Add orange juice, salt and pepper; bring to a boil. Reduce heat to low, and cook, uncovered, 2 minutes.

3 Place broccoli in large bowl. Pour orange sauce over broccoli, and toss well. Serve hot.

Per Serving: 80 cal; 5g prot; 3.5g total fat (0.5g sat. fat); 11g carb; 0mg chol; 220mg sod; 4g fiber; 3g sugars

Chocolate Bean Cupcakes

MAKES 12 CUPCAKES

Your kids will never guess these protein-packed snacks are good for them!

15 minutes | 30 minutes | **45** minutes

CUPCAKES

1¼ cups granulated sugar

2 large eggs, or ½ cup egg substitute

⅓ cup soy margarine, melted

One 15.5-ounce can black beans, drained, rinsed and puréed

2 tablespoons grated orange zest, optional

2 teaspoons pure vanilla extract

1 cup all-purpose flour

½ cup cocoa powder

2 teaspoons baking powder

FROSTING

½ cup soy margarine

2 cups confectioners' sugar

4 tablespoons frozen orange juice concentrate, thawed

Food coloring, for tinting, optional

12 chocolate Kisses

1 Preheat oven to 375°F. Line 12 cupcake wells with baking liners.

2 *To make Cupcakes:* Beat sugar, eggs and margarine using electric mixer on high, 3 minutes, or until thick and creamy.

3 Put puréed beans into large bowl, and fold in orange zest, if using, and vanilla extract.

4 Whisk together flour, cocoa powder and baking powder in small bowl.

5 Fold egg mixture into beans, then fold flour mixture into beans in thirds. Fill cupcake baking liners two-thirds full. Bake 20 minutes, or until toothpick inserted in center comes out clean. Cool in pan 5 minutes. Remove, and cool on rack.

6 *Meanwhile, to make Frosting:* Beat margarine until smooth using electric mixer. Beat in confectioners' sugar, then juice concentrate until smooth. If too stiff, add 1 teaspoon water at a time. Tint with food coloring, if using. Top each cupcake with 2 teaspoons frosting and a chocolate Kiss.

Per Cupcake: 385 cal; 5g prot; 15g total fat (4g sat. fat); 60g carb; 35mg chol; 280mg sod; 3g fiber; 44g sugars

cooking methods

Baking: Baking refers to cooking food with dry heat in an oven. If you plan to bake or roast, always preheat the oven before you begin preparing the recipe; otherwise the oven won't be ready when you are.

When you bake more than one thing at a time, stagger the placement of the dishes so that air may circulate, and if a recipe calls for baking a dish on a rack placed in the center of the oven, follow those directions. Also keep in mind that few ovens are calibrated accurately, and they may cook slower or faster than you anticipate. A good way to check your oven's accuracy is to use an oven thermometer and to check the cooking time.

Blanching: Quickly dipping fruits or vegetables into boiling water and then putting them into cold water for a few seconds loosens skins, sets color and readies them for freezing or for further cooking using another technique, such as stir-frying. You also may blanch nuts, but skip the cold-water dunk. To remove the skins, rub the nuts between your fingertips or with a clean kitchen towel.

Braising: This traditional French method of cooking vegetables in a little butter or oil and liquid in a covered pot over low heat. Braising makes for richly flavored dishes.

Broiling: Simply set your oven on the broil setting and place your broiler-safe dish or pan on the broiling rack at the height called for in your recipe. In vegetarian cooking, broiling is primarily for melting cheese on casseroles or for top browning.

Deep-frying: Fill a pot one-third full of vegetable oil—not olive oil or butter, which both have a low smoke point—and heat it to 375°F. Do not let the oil smoke, as it may burn. Use a deep-fat thermometer to help regulate the temperature. Make sure that the food you are deep-frying is in small pieces and is dry— moisture in food, especially raw vegetables, can cause hot oil to spatter. Another option is to coat the food with a batter.

Use a wire basket or slotted spoon to lower and lift your food into and out of the oil, and fry only small amounts of food at a time. If you add too much food at once, you will reduce the temperature of the oil and end up with soggy, greasy food. For that same reason, do not deep-fry frozen foods or foods that are colder than room temperature. Cook vegetables coated with batter about 3 to 5 minutes, until they are crisp and lightly browned. Drain fried foods on paper towels and serve immediately.

Grilling: Your backyard gas or charcoal barbecue is a handy piece of equipment for anyone who likes to infuse his food with extra flavor—and to cook outdoors. Once you buy a small-meshed basket or screen to fit over the grilling rack, you can grill any number of vegetables and fruits—plus veggie burgers— without fear of losing them to the flames below. You may also want to invest in a long-handled spatula, a long-handled brush for basting and appropriate hot pads for lifting the cooking racks off the grill.

Stovetop grilling: Many modern ovens have grilling inserts set into their stovetops, and these grills give the cook the chance to approximate outdoor grilling flavor while staying indoors and avoiding the fuss. Follow the manufacturer's directions for your particular unit.

Pan-frying: If you want to fry vegetables, pan-frying is probably the easiest method. Choose a metal pan with sides high enough to hold the food and enough cooking oil or fats to cover about one-half the thickness of the food. This way you can cook the food throughout with only one turn. Because pan-frying involves high temperatures, you cannot pan-fry with butter, margarine or olive oil; they will smoke and burn. Use vegetable oil instead.

Poaching: Cooking vegetables, fruits and eggs in simmering water or vegetable stock can produce flavorful results in a short time without added calories from fat. Adding vinegar to the poaching water when cooking eggs helps set the whites.

Puréeing: Puréeing involves turning ingredients such as fruits or vegetables into a thick, uniformly smooth paste. You may use a food mill, blender or food processor to purée. If you want to purée hot liquids in a blender, check that you have a heatproof container. Fill the blender no more than half full, and hold the lid in place with a thick towel.

Roasting: Roasting, like baking, uses dry oven heat to cook the food; the food remains uncovered during cooking. To keep the food from drying out or charring during roasting, you may brush it with oil to keep the surface moist. To prevent the top of the food from becoming too brown, create a loose tent of aluminum foil over the top to protect the surface while still allowing hot air to circulate underneath. Keep in mind that smaller pieces of food can become very dry when roasted and may be better suited for pan-frying or broiling.

Sautéing: Sautéing involves quick-cooking foods in a small amount of butter or oil over medium to medium-high heat. It's similar to the Chinese technique of stir-frying but generally is used for larger pieces of food.

Simmering: A liquid simmers when heated over low heat and tiny bubbles just begin to break the surface.

Steaming: Steaming vegetables makes them crisp-tender. Fill a saucepan with about 1 inch of water and set a steamer basket in the pan. Bring the water to a boil, and add rinsed vegetables to the basket. Reduce the heat to medium-low, cover the pan and cook until the vegetables reach the desired doneness. Time varies depending on the vegetable, but often just a few minutes will be enough. The big plus: Because the vegetables do not touch the water, their vitamin and mineral content does not leach into the water.

Stir-frying: Stir-frying is a method of quick-cooking vegetables over high heat while constantly stirring them. You may use a wok, but a skillet or other pan works fine, too. A wok has a rounded bottom, which gets the hottest, and sloping sides that remain cooler. The differences in heat allow you to cook the ingredients evenly by rearranging the food. For stirring, you may use a wooden spoon, but a Chinese-style spatula is best.

index

Scramble, Curried Tofu, 14
Sesame
  -Ginger Tofu with Asparagus and
    Shiitakes, 127
  Tofu Salad, Chilled, with Ginger,
    Green Onions, Asparagus
    and, 31
  Wonton Wedges, 46
Seville Burgers with Olive-Orange
  Relish, 21
Shake
  Creamy Wake-Up, 189
  Milk, Sunny Strawberry, 188
Shiitake(s)
  and Asparagus, Ginger-Sesame Tofu
    with, 127
  -Spinach Salad, 70
Shirataki Noodle-Broccoli Soup, 94
Simple Syrup, 190
Singapore-Style Rice Noodles with
  Snow Peas, Peppers, Cabbage
  and Tofu, 151
Slaw, 141
  Mardi Gras, 103
  Red Cabbage, with Baked Tofu and
    Peanut Dressing, 76
Sloppy Joes, Spicy, 26
Snack Mix, Nutty, 198
Snow Peas
  in Chinese Vegetables and Hoisin-
    Braised Tempeh, 137
  Rice Noodles with Peppers, Cabbage,
    Tofu and, Singapore-Style, 151
  in Tempeh with Coconut Milk and
    Lemongrass, 136
  with Tofu and Cashews, Gingered, 131
Soba Noodles
  Broccoli, Two-, Stir-Fry on, 149
  Thai-Style Tofu and, 150
Soda, Strawberry-Orange, Old-
  Fashioned, 190
Soufflés, Ricotta, with Mixed Berry
  Compote, 180
Soup(s)
  Asparagus, "Cream" of, 91
  Bean, Three-, 87
  Black Bean, with Roasted Red
    Pepper, 85
  Broccoli-Shirataki Noodle, 94
  Carrot, with Asparagus and Pastina, 95
  Cauliflower and Leek Potage, 97
  Miso, with Vegetables, Steaming, 93
  Pumpkin-Coconut Bisque, 92
  Spinach-Potato, Curried, 96
  White Bean, with Collard Greens, 86
Soybean. See also Edamame
  Black, Tabbouleh, 32
Soy Cheese
  American Sandwich, Grilled, 17
  in Burrito, All-Day, 25

Cheddar-Lime Dressing, Creamy, 55
  in Panini, Mexican-Style, 202
Quesadillas, Spinach-Tempeh, 22
Scones, Asparagus, 4
  in Zucchini "Fettuccine" with Fresh
    Marinara, 159
Soy "Chicken" Chow Mein, 170
Soy "Ice Cream" Sundae, Persian, 181
Soy "Meatballs" and Couscous,
  Moroccan, 167
Soy "Meat" Crumbles
  in Chili and Polenta Casserole, 162
  in Curry and Chickpea Lettuce
    Wraps, 27
  in Gravy, Home-Style, Mashed
    Potatoes with, 166
  Hummus with "Ground Meat",
    Onions and Toasted Pine
    Nuts, 35
  in Sloppy Joes, Spicy, 26
  in Sweet Potato Hash, Hearty, 7
  in Tostadas, Easy, 201
Soy "Sausage"
  in American Sandwich, Grilled, 17
  Black-Eyed Pea Stew with Kale,
    Butternut Squash and, 89
  in Pizza, Breakfast, 10
  with Potatoes, Skillet, 8
Spinach
  in Artichoke Dip, Hot, 36
  Couscous, with BBQ Tofu, 133
  Eggplant and Potato Curry with
    Cilantro and, 141
  -Lentil Stew, Lemony, 99
  -Potato Soup, Curried, 96
  and Roasted Red Pepper Sauce,
    Creamy, Pasta with, 155
  Salad, and Blue Cheese, 57
  Salad, Extra-Healthy, 56
  Salad, -Shiitake, 70
  -Tempeh Quesadillas, 22
  with Tofu, Garlicky, over Pasta, 152
Spreads. See Dips and Spreads
Squash. See Butternut Squash; Yellow
  Squash; Zucchini
Stew(s)
  Black-Eyed Pea, with Kale, Butternut
    Squash and Soy "Sausage", 89
  Chickpea Ragoût, Warm, with Swiss
    Chard, Carrots and Harissa, 134
  Corn and Mushrooms, A Little Stew
    of, 116
  Eggplant and Fennel, Mediterranean,
    98
  Lentil-Spinach, Lemony, 99
  Vegetable Ragoût, Tuscan, 100
Strawberry
  Milk Shake, Sunny, 188
  -Orange Soda, Old-Fashioned, 190
  Salad with Gorgonzola Dressing, 59

Succotash, Edamame, 109
Sugar Snap Pea(s)
  Almondine, 112
  Summer Rolls, 30
Summer Pasta Salad with Grilled
  Vegetables, 82
Summer Rolls
  Salad, with Spicy Peanut Dressing, 165
  Sugar Snap Pea, 30
Sundae, Persian "Ice Cream", 181
Sweet Potato(es)
  Hash, Hearty, 7
  Salad, Grilled, 81
  in Skillet Potatoes with Soy "Sausage", 8
  in Vegetable-Lentil Curry, 139
Swiss Chard
  Chickpea Ragoût, Warm, with
    Carrots, Harissa and, 134
  -Potato Toss, 119
  -Tahini Sauce, Garlicky, over
    Quinoa, 120
  and White Beans, Garlicky, with
    Pasta, 153
Syrup
  Balsamic, Baked Tomato and
    Mozzarella Stacks with
    Arugula, Corn and, 78
  Ginger, in Mango-Ginger Pudding,
    176
  Simple, 190

T

Tabbouleh
  Black Soybean, 32
  Bulgur and Lentil Salad, Fruited, 74
  Quinoa, 73
Tacos, Chipotle Black Bean, with
  Roasted Butternut Squash, 23
Tahini
  -Chard Sauce, Garlicky, over Quinoa,
    120
  in Gravy, Home-Style, Mashed
    Potatoes with, 166
  in Hummus, Edamame, 34
Tart
  Lemon, Instant, 183
  Pepper, Late-Summer Crustless, 144
Tea Sandwiches, Herbed Goat Cheese
  and Cucumber, 47
Tempeh
  in "Bolognese" Sauce, Vegetable
    Linguine with, 156-157
  with Coconut Milk and Lemongrass,
    136
  Hoisin-Braised, and Chinese
    Vegetables, 137
  -Spinach Quesadillas, 22
  Triangles with Piccata Sauce, 135
Thai Rice Pancakes, 29
Thai-Style Tofu and Noodles, 150